LIFE and DOCTRINE

How the TRUTH *and* GRACE *of the Christian story* CHANGE *everything*

ADAM MABRY

Life and Doctrine: How the Truth and Grace of the Christian Story Change Everything
Copyright 2014, 2017 Adam Mabry
Published by Aletheia Resources
Aletheia Resources
820 Massachusetts Avenue
Cambridge, MA, 02139,United States
www.aletheia.org

ISBN: 978-1-312-24685-0

All rights reserved. No part of this publication may be reproduced, stored in a retrieval system, or transmitted in any form by any means, electronic, mechanical, photocopy, recording or otherwise, without the prior permission of the publisher, except as provided for by USA copyright law.

Unless otherwise indicated, Scripture quotations are taken from the ESV Bible (The Holy Bible: English Standard Version). Copyright 2001 by Crossway Bibles, a publishing ministry of Good News Publishers. Used by permission. All rights reserved.

TABLE OF CONTENTS

Prelude — 4

Section 1: Truth

    Knowing — 14
    Words — 29
    God — 45

Section 2: Grace

    Origin — 65
    Redemption — 85
    Rescue — 106

Section 3: Change

    Being — 130
    Church — 144
    Hope — 159

Postlude — 175

PRELUDE

WHY

Prelude – Why

THE QUESTION WE'RE ALL ASKING

I was kind of an annoying kid.

Some kids whine, some manipulate, some won't pay attention. None of these were my particular specialty, though. I would ask "why" all the time. No really, all the time.

I remember being about four years old, riding in the car with my mother on the way to daycare and asking, "Mom, why do you watch the news?" She looked at me, puzzled, but acquiesced. The following morning, I again asked her, "Mom, why do you watch the news?" She looked at me oddly, but, laughing it off, answered again.

Next day. Same car. Same question.

"Adam," she responded, "you've asked me the same question for three days. I already answered, don't you remember?"

"Yeah, I remember," I said, "but I wanted to see if the reason was still the same." I feel annoyed at myself just recalling the story.

Thankfully (or at least hopefully) my social graces have matured somewhat, but I still never quite got past my fixation on the question of "why?" I suppose I've always believed that everything has a reason, a purpose. When I got the inspiration to write this book, I first had to answer my own favorite question – why?

So why did I write this book? Three reasons should sum it up nicely.

First, we are living in a cultural milieu whose basic mental posture toward religious matters is doubt. Doubt everything. You heard someone saw a ghost? Doubt it. A friend you know converted to some religion? Doubt him. Someone is praying for you? Doubt that'll work. There is a knee-jerk reaction in the Western soul to doubt, well, everything.

Now, let me be the first to say that there are some good reasons to doubt. After all, it can't all be true, can it? Haven't we seen enough news specials about mind-control cults, religious nut jobs, preachers who take too much money, priests who commit unspeakable acts toward kids, religious terrorists, and a host of others to make us all prefer to simply stay home on Sundays? Watch enough 20/20 specials on religion and you'll soon feel pretty settled that doubt is safe – or at least safer than belief.

Another good reason to doubt is because it has been the default posture of Western culture for about three hundred years. Ever since the cultural and intellectual movement known as the Enlightenment, it's part of the tradition of Western experience to doubt an idea until it proves itself worthy of belief, which brings me to the first reason I wrote this book.

The Christian story is worth believing.

DOUBT YOUR WAY AHEAD

I believe the Christian story is worth building your whole life upon. Perhaps that sounds crazy to you. Perhaps you have honest doubts about the Christian story. Maybe it's the existence of God in particular which troubles you, or the whole idea of being able to know anything for sure. Perhaps you've known church folk who seemed nothing but hypocrites. Whatever your particular doubt is, let me encourage you – go on doubting.

Why would a pastor like me encourage you to persist in doubt? Isn't my job to wrangle you into belief by whatever means necessary? In his book *The Reason for God*, Tim Keller points out that doubts are never alone, but the other side of the coin of belief. Behind every doubt about the Christian story, there is an alternate belief. He says,

> *You cannot doubt Belief A except from a position of faith in Belief B. For example, if you doubt Christianity because "There can't just be one true religion," you must recognize that this statement is itself an act of faith. No one can prove it empirically, and it is not a universal truth that everyone accepts. If you went to the middle east and said [that], nearly everyone would say, "Why not?" The reason you doubt Christianity's Belief A is because you hold unprovable Belief B. Every doubt, therefore, is based on a leap of faith.*[1]

Your doubts about the Christian story aren't alone. They are accompanied by beliefs. You doubt because you currently believe something that makes belief in the Christian story difficult, if not impossible. Therefore, my encouragement to you is not to stop doubting, but to doubt more. In fact, why not try doubting your doubts?

If you really want to know ultimate reality (or at least, want to enough to pick up this book), then you must be honest enough to at least apply the same rigorous standards of doubt to your own doubts that you apply to Christianity. Isn't that fair?

So, I would like to invite you *not* to lobotomize yourself and merely agree with me. I want to invite you to doubt more fully and more forcefully. The way I see it, the worst that could happen is you become a better, more honest skeptic. But the best that could happen … well the best that could happen is better than you could possibly imagine.

FROM INFORMATION TO TRANSFORMATION

It is my observation that whatever we say we believe, there is often a gap between our confession and our experience. I want to eliminate that gap. The gap may be there because our beliefs are false. So, the first section of this book will deal with those foundational beliefs – those doctrines – which act like the concrete under our lives. My hope is that by standing upon the truths of the Christian story, you will move from the realm of your mind alone as these doctrines enter your experience – truth touching life. The gap between doctrine and life will narrow. The Bible has a word for this: grace. Have you ever known something as factually true, but failed to let that knowledge shape your life? Someone may agree with the statement, "God

---
[1] Tim Keller, *The Reason for God*. New York, NY: Dutton, 2008, xvii.

Prelude – Why

exists," or "I should follow Jesus," but that statement of belief, for some reason, never makes its way into real life. There's a gap between their lives and the doctrines they profess.

Sometimes, the longest distance in the world is the space between the head and the heart – between agreement and action.

The second reason I wrote this book was to help Christians who are self-aware enough to see that there's a gulf between their statement of faith and the way they live. I don't merely desire to help you agree with the truthfulness of Christianity; I desire you to develop a solid foundation upon which to build your life. Truths are agreed with; grace is embraced. I really do believe that the Christian story is worth believing, not just agreeing with. So, the second section – grace – will form the next leg of our bridge. The Christian story is one that isn't content to remain in the realm of hypotheticals. Much like the God it describes, the story wants to resonate with your real, daily life.

So while I do want you to agree with what I believe are the truths of the gospel, I hope you'll go a step further and see them applied to your life.

WHAT IF WE COULD KNOW GOD?

This brings us to the final reason for this book, and the final facet of the Christian story – change. Change is a powerful idea. Promise of change motivates us to work hard. Hope of change inspires us to believe passionately. Lack of change depresses us deeply. If we really know Truth – know God – then we'll change. We'll have to. The Christian Scriptures themselves tell us that their story has within it the power to change us – to renew us.

When a first-century, ragtag group of nobodies experienced the truth and grace of the gospel, they were radically changed. In fact, the whole course of human history was, too.

Perhaps you're already a Christian. You don't have many doubts about the truthfulness of the story. You may not have any at all. Your problem is different – you've been inspired by preaching, sung the songs, attended church services, but you've never really been changed. You know right doctrine, but somehow you feel like you've missed out on knowing God. I hope that changes. If it does, and you're able to see the story anew – the story of the truth, grace, and changing power of the gospel – then our bridge will be complete.

Isaiah had an experience like this. He records a vision where he was taken up into Heaven, and he laid eyes on ultimate reality – God himself. Here's the story in Isaiah's own words,

> *In the year that King Uzziah died I saw the Lord sitting upon a throne, high and lifted up; and the train of his robe filled the temple. Above him stood the seraphim. Each had six wings: with two he covered his face, and with two he covered his feet, and with two he flew. And one called to another and said:*
>
> *"Holy, holy, holy is the LORD of hosts;*
> *the whole earth is full of his glory!"*

And the foundations of the thresholds shook at the voice of him who called, and the house was filled with smoke. And I said: "Woe is me! For I am lost; for I am a man of unclean lips, and I dwell in the midst of a people of unclean lips; for my eyes have seen the King, the LORD of hosts!"

Then one of the seraphim flew to me, having in his hand a burning coal that he had taken with tongs from the altar. And he touched my mouth and said: "Behold, this has touched your lips; your guilt is taken away ..." (Isaiah 6:1-7).

To modern ears this story sounds like fiction ... and weird fiction at that. Angels with six wings? Coals on the lips?

But new truth is always a bit jarring, isn't it? How much more jarring are new truths about God when they happen upon us? Consider some of the truths that were hitting Isaiah: *God exists. God is bigger and brighter than I imagined. He's surrounded with these crazy looking angels ...* If it sounds crazy for us to read, it must've been even stranger for him to experience. Did God look different from what he imagined? Did this all fit into his tidy view of the world?

The fact is, it didn't matter. Meeting God means meeting him on *his* terms. When the truth of God – his reality, presence, power – burst into Isaiah's consciousness, he was overwhelmed with wonder ... and with woe.

This fantastic interruption from God left Isaiah with at least two distinct impressions: God is greater than I imagined him to be, and I am less than I would've liked to admit.

"I am unclean – my mouth, my people, my family – we're all broken. I'm not worthy to be here!" he cried out.

We live in a self-esteem culture. Guidance counsellors everywhere would be shocked to hear a pupil say such things. Negative self-talk is quickly hushed up because it damages self-esteem, self-worth, and self-actualization – so we're told. After all, Isaiah was a good guy, right? I mean, he was a prophet! He was a religious guy. He never hurt anyone. In fact, he was sleeping in the temple when he had this vision!

But just because we dislike saying something doesn't make it false. Compared to other people, Isaiah measured up pretty well. But he wasn't in the room with other people. He was in the room with God. God reached down out of Heaven and pulled Isaiah up into his throne room. Compared to God, Isaiah immediately saw how much he didn't measure up. Yet, despite Isaiah's unworthiness, God still invited him.

Graciously, God invites us, too.

The truth about God overwhelmed Isaiah with awareness of God's greatness and his own unworthiness. Then a strange thing happened. One of the angels took tongs and, removing a coal from the fire, touched it against Isaiah's mouth. God, recognizing the problem with Isaiah – namely that his mouth and life weren't clean – makes up the difference. He purifies Isaiah, and makes him able to know him, and to be known by him.

Did you catch it? Truth. Grace. Change.

Truth: God is great. Isaiah is not.

Grace: Despite Isaiah's unworthiness, God wants to know him.

Prelude – Why

Change: God purifies Isaiah, knows Isaiah, and Isaiah knows God.

After Isaiah met God, he was changed forever. His perspective changed. His purpose changed. His trajectory changed. He even became an agent for change in a world desperate for it. Everything else we know about Isaiah, everything else he ever did or said, we can trace back to this one, life-transforming collision of truth and grace, changing him forever. That's my hope for you. Whether you're coming to this book with serious doubts and concerns, or you're coming to this book with inconsistencies and problems, my hope is that you'll consider the possibility that the truth of the Christian story contains the power to introduce you to God. Once you meet God, everything changes.

To get the most out of this book I recommend looking the Scriptures up on your own, and taking time to read them before and after. Also, have a look at the Study Guide; interacting with the text will make the experience not only informative, but applicable to your life.

Finally, I'd like to ask you to read what follows prayerfully. Perhaps you're not a person who prays a lot, or perhaps you are. In any case, God has made a promise that, if we would ask, he would actually illuminate his truth and grace to us. So ask. You may be surprised to find you actually receive.

APPLICATION & REFLECTION

1. Read Isaiah 6:1-7. What stands out as significant to you?

   _____
   _____
   _____

2. Why are you reading this book? What do you want to get out of it?

   _____
   _____
   _____

Prelude – Why

SECTION ONE

TRUTH

Knowing – **Chapter One**

CHAPTER ONE

KNOWING

DOUBTS, DOUBTS EVERYWHERE

There's a difference between healthy skepticism and unhealthy cynicism.

Skepticism is doubting everything until you're convinced by something. It's this healthy level of doubt which keeps the bad ideas out. In this way, the Apostle Paul was a skeptic. He said, "but test everything; hold fast what is good" (1 Thes. 5:21). Cynicism, on the other hand, is the refusal to believe anything. Doubt like that keeps even the good ideas out, too.

Cynicism is doubting everyone because you believe nothing is convincing – the belief that nothing is to be believed. But if the cynic is determined to believe that nothing is to be believed, isn't that a belief? Perhaps the cynic should be cynical of his own cynicism. C. S. Lewis makes this observation in *The Abolition of Man*,

> *You cannot go on 'seeing through' things forever. The whole point of seeing through something is to see something through it. It is good that the window should be transparent, because the street or garden beyond is opaque. How if you saw through the garden too? It is no use trying to 'see through' first principles. If you see through everything, then everything is transparent. But a wholly transparent world is an invisible world. To 'see through' all things is the same as not to see.*[2]

For Lewis, knowing involves some "first principles."

You exist.

Others exist.

The past actually happened.

The laws of nature work everywhere.

We all believe those last four sentences, but there's no way to prove them. Philosopher Alvin Plantinga wants to press us further and tell us that belief in God is basic, foundational – a starting place. And more amazingly, he argues that you're perfectly justified in believing in God without any additional proof at all![3]

There are some beliefs you believe because of other beliefs. For instance, I believe that my refrigerator will keep my food cold. I believe that because I have a vague awareness of how fridges work. I also believe that because I paid my power bill this month. So, as far as I understand fridges to work, and as far as I trust my power company to maintain my electricity service, I'm pretty well justified in believing that my fridge will keep my food cold. I believe all that stuff about my food staying cold on that basis of those other beliefs. But not all beliefs are like this. As I write this, I believe that I've got a slight headache. I don't believe that on the basis of another belief. I don't have an argument for it. It's just apparent. My head hurts. I can't not be aware of my headache. Scoff all you like, but it's true.

---

[2] C.S. Lewis. *The Abolition of Man*. 53-54

[3] See Alvin Plantinga, *Warranted Christian Belief*. Oxford University Press: UK, 2000.

But let's go back to my fridge for a moment. I believe it will keep my food cold. That's because I know how it works, and I know my power is working. So far this all sounds very rational – belief in fridges based upon science. But at the bottom of that chain of "I believe this because I believe that," are a few very simple, basic beliefs. I believe I exist. I believe the outside world exists. I can't prove those things, but I simply can't not be aware of their truthfulness.

Similarly, awareness of God's existence is, for Lewis and Plantinga at least, not a conclusion you get to at the end of a long argument. For them, it's the belief in God that starts the discussion in the first place. It sounds strange to us, but this is hardly a new idea. John Calvin talked about it half a millennium ago in his own writing. He liked to call it the *sensus divinitatis*, or "awareness of the Divine."

> *There is within the human mind, and indeed by natural instinct, an awareness of divinity. This we take to be beyond controversy. . . [T]his conviction, namely, that there is some God, is naturally inborn in all, and is fixed deep within, as it were in the very marrow.*[4]

To quote Lewis again, "I believe in Christianity as I believe that the Sun has risen. Not only because I see it, but because by it I see everything else."[5]

Let's be clear about what he's not saying. Lewis isn't saying that there aren't good reasons to believe in God. There certainly are, and we'll come to a few of those in a moment. But for now, let's consider the strange possibility that without belief in God, a whole host of things become, well, unbelievable.

What does Psalm 19:1 tell us about how we can know God?

we need to lower our belief system.

HAS SCIENCE DISPROVED GOD?

Most scientifically-minded atheists have become firmly convinced that science has discredited God's very existence, or at least rendered God explanatorily unnecessary. To those of this persuasion, knowing God is a foolish pursuit, because there's no God

---

[4] John Calvin, *Institutes of the Christian Religion* (Philadelphia: Westminster Press, 1960), 43, 45-46.

[5] C.S. Lewis, *Weight of Glory*, "Is Theology Poetry?"

there to know. Apostle of this new atheism, Richard Dawkins, says, "Faith is the great cop-out, the great excuse to evade the need to think and evaluate evidence. Faith is belief in spite of, even perhaps because of, the lack of evidence."[6]

There are a few problems with Dawkins' quote, not the least of which is the fact that he, as a biologist at the prestigious Oxford University, uses faith assumptions all the time. Every time Professor Dawkins is in the lab, he assumes that the biological world is able to be understood. He assumes that the laws of nature will be consistent – that gravity won't just turn off one day. He assumes the world is rational and intelligible. But can he prove it? What possible experiment could be done to show that the universe is able to be experimented upon?

None. These are articles of faith – those properly basic, first principles.

Of course, this isn't at all to demean science. I'm typing on a computer right now. I've got a smartphone. I've been treated at a hospital. I'm a fan of science and all its tangible benefits. I'm not a fan, however, of making science into the source of all knowledge. Plantinga also notes,

> *Some treat science as if it were a sort of infallible oracle ... Many look to scientists for guidance on matters outside of science, matters on which scientists have no special expertise. They apparently think of scientists as the new priestly class; unsurprisingly, scientists don't ordinarily discourage this tendency.*[7]

But without God, the scientific enterprise can't even get off the ground. Without God, there's no reason to believe that there's any kind of universal, law-like rhyme or reason to the world around us. Where I live in Boston, I'm surrounded by some of the world's greatest universities. For hundreds of years, people in my city have committed time, talent, and treasure to better understanding the world.

But if humans are, as Bertrand Russell stated, "merely the collocations of random atoms," then how is it that we come to understand each other and the world around us? Matter is dumb. If humans are merely more complex arrangements of matter, then how do we make sense of knowing anything? We are merely more complicated versions of chairs, rocks, and ficus trees. To quote another Oxford man, Dr. John Lennox, "You've got to believe in the rational intelligibility of the universe before you can do any science at all. Science doesn't give you that."[8]

In summary, science only works because the world is orderly and rational. Science can't explain why science works. Only God can, because only God is big enough to ground the rational intelligibility upon which science depends.

It seems to me that if you jettison God, then you lose any underlying assurance that the world is reasonable, law-governed, or knowable. But if you accept that God created the world around you, you'll of assume that it reflects some aspects of his nature – order, reason, and even beauty. Early scientists seem to have no problem understanding this. Isaac Newton said, "The wonderful arrangement and harmony of the cosmos would only originate in the plan of an almighty omniscient being. This is and remains my greatest comprehension." Copernicus echoes a similar sentiment when he says, "Through steady observation and a meaningful contact with the divined order of the world's structure, arranged by God's wisdom – who would not be guided to admire the Builder who creates all!" These early scientists, whose discoveries form the foundations of much modern

---

[6] Richard Dawkins, Untitled Lecture, Edinburgh Science Festival, 1992.

[7] Alvin Plantinga, *Where the Conflict Really Lies: Science, Religion, and Naturalism* (Oxford, 2011) 18.

[8] John Lennox. The God Delusion Debate, hosted by Fixed Point Foundation. Birmingham, AL, 2006.

science, seemed to understand this with no problem at all. So, either they were double-minded, stupid, or they were simply acknowledging the foundation upon which all science stands – rationality, order, and intelligibility. All features which are only explicable if the universe was created to be this way.

More recently, other great scientific minds have echoed the sentiments of their forefathers. Dr. William Lane Craig, professor of philosophy at Talbot School of Theology, makes the observation in an interview with *Time*:

> *In a quiet revolution in thought and argument that hardly anybody could have foreseen only two decades ago, God is making a comeback. Most intriguingly, this is happening not among theologians or ordinary believers, but in the crisp intellectual circles of academic philosophers, where the consensus had long banished the Almighty from fruitful discourse.*[9]

Paul Davies, theoretical physicist and one of the most influential expositors of modern science agrees, saying,

> *Science is based on the assumption [on faith!] that the universe is thoroughly rational and logical at all levels ... Atheists claim that the laws [of nature] exist reasonlessly and that the universe is ultimately absurd. As a scientist, I find this hard to accept. There must be an unchanging rational ground in which the logical, orderly nature of the universe is rooted.*[10]

Just a few short years ago, the academic world was rocked when leading atheist philosopher Antony Flew announced that he changed his mind about his atheism. So, what key piece of insight seemed to turn the tide in his thinking after decades of prolific writing and thinking for atheism?

> *Why do I believe this, given that I expounded and defended atheism for more than a half century? The short answer is this: this is the world picture, as I see it, that has emerged from modern science. Science spotlights three dimensions of nature that point to God. The first is the fact that nature obeys laws. The second is the dimension of life, of intelligently organized and purpose-driven being, which arose from matter. The third is the very existence of nature.*[11]

It seems to me that attempting to do science involves a great deal of faith in all sorts of unprovable assumptions; assumptions which only make sense if they're rooted in something beyond the laws of nature – a lawgiver.

Can science disprove God? What can science do?

_____

_____

_____

---

[9] William Lane Craig, "Modernizing the Case for God," *Time*, April 7, 1980, pp. 65- 6.

[10] Paul Davies, "What Happened Before the Big Bang?" in *God for the 21st Century*, ed. Russell Stannard (Philadelphia: Templeton Foundation Press, 2000), 12.

[11] Antony Flew, *There is a God,* (New York, NY: HarperCollins, 2007), 88-9.

IT'S WRONG TO SAY YOU KNOW GOD

What I've just done there is to quickly jot out a good reason to believe in God. But not all objections to faith are so rationalistic. There is another kind of objection, often called a postmodern one. It's the idea that when someone claims to know "the truth," what they're after isn't wisdom, knowledge, or a relationship with God. What they're really after is power.[12] This goes for religious people too. And some of us are pretty convinced that when someone says they "know God," they're acting immorally or even dangerously. Postmodern philosopher Denis Diderot famously said, "Men will never be free until that last king is strangled on the entrails of the last priest."[13] As a pastor, I sure hope he's wrong.[14]

I can certainly understand why some may believe this. When the attacks of September 11, 2001 happened in New York City, news commentators were quick to point out the dangers of a group of people who were fanatically committed to the idea that they alone knew the truth. It wasn't long before anyone who claimed to have the truth (mainly religious people, anyway) were either laughed off as lunatics, mere steps away from blowing themselves up for their own causes, or decried as moral monsters, philosophically empowering their followers to pull off the next 9/11.

Another reason this claim appears attractive is because our culture has been hurt by guys like, well, me – religious leaders who've been entrusted with the care and moral protection of society. How many more headline news stories do we need to read about men in my own line of work who end up sleeping with their secretary, stealing money from the church, or doing unspeakable acts of violence to the weakest among us. Such examples of the abuse of power have caused many in our culture to imagine that when we pastor-types claim we know truth, power is all we're after to begin with.

This may surprise you, but this objection wasn't first sounded by hippie philosophy students, but by Jesus. This was the same accusation that Jesus leveled against the Pharisees (the religious leaders who ended up planning his murder). He said of them, "[They] tie up heavy burdens, hard to bear, and lay them on people's shoulders, but they themselves are not willing to move them with their finger." (Matt. 23:4). There were those, even in his day, who would use their claim to divine knowledge – to truth – to manipulate and gain power over the masses. That's repulsive, or at least it was to Jesus.

Let me say again, I understand why this objection resonates with so many. But, as I indicated earlier, I don't think that one can make this assumption and at the same time deny God's existence. To say "it's wrong to say you know God (or truth)," you have to overcome two problems ... problems that, it seems to me, cannot be resolved without God.

First is the problem of the claim itself. Imagine that I, as a pastor, come to you one day and say, "God loves you and has sent his only Son into the world to die on a cross for your sins. He's provided a way for your spiritual rescue and you should repent of your life, works, and thoughts and follow Jesus wholeheartedly." Then, you reply, "You insensitive jerk! Who are you to tell me that you know God, or that you know what I should do!? No one can say they have the truth. It's people like you who think the God they supposedly know told them to fly planes into buildings and blow up abortion clinics."

---

[12] Such observations really began with Friedrich Nietzsche, who claimed that deep within us lies *der wille zür macht* – the will to power. This is the idea that each of us are consumed with gaining power and prominence over others.

[13] Denis Diderot, attributed by Jean-François de La Harpe in *Cours de Littérature Ancienne et Moderne* (1840)

[14] Giving credit where it's due, I have to say that I heard that joke in a Tim Keller sermon. I still laugh at it.

Now, before I attempt to answer that objection, try to feel the weight of it. It's a passionately held position, and with good reason. It's true that there have been those in the world who claim to know God deeply who then go on to do terrible acts in his name. But think about this with me for a minute. You have just told me that no one should say that they have the truth. How is that not a claim to truth? Haven't you simply uttered with one sentence what you rejected with another? In logic, we like to call this little fallacy the violation of the law of non-contradiction. To say or believe that no one should claim to know the truth is itself a claim to truth. If we give the universal principle, "No one should claim that they've got the truth," then we've just made a claim to a universal truth.

Oops.

But there's an additional problem. Here in the West in the 21st century, we are committed to the idea that no one should impose his or her view of ultimate reality on another. We are told that it is wrong to impose our vision of morality, beauty, or goodness on another. That may or may not be true, but the truthfulness of that idea isn't what I'm concerned about at this point. What's interesting to me is how implicitly moral and religious our cultural rejection seems to be.

This isn't the only implicitly moral belief that pervades our society. There are others – religion and public life should be separate, society should care for its weaker members, we should tolerate those of different beliefs and backgrounds, etc. None of these are statements of the way things are, these are statements about the way things ought to be. That places them squarely in the category of morality. But on what basis should we believe any of this to be true?

Any claim to a universal "ought" like, "you ought not say you know the truth," is a moral statement. It seems to me impossible, however, to make any such claims without God. Who among us has the right to make a moral claim on all of us? Without a divine lawgiver, how is it actually wrong to do anything? It surely can't be because our culture thinks so. There are many cultures in the world today that do not share our cultural convictions. Are we then to say that our cultural "oughts" are better than theirs? If we do, then we become guilty of the very claim we hate: the claim to a universal truth.

To say that claims to know the truth are wrong, one must be able to say what is, in fact, wrong. One must import God's ideas of actual, objective moral standards and God's moral vocabulary to just deny knowledge about him.

Read Proverbs 14:12, 16:2, 21:2, and 26:12. What do these verses have to say about the objection above?
_____
_____
_____

GOD IN THE PROBLEMS

Both these objections to God's existence seem to create far more problems than they attempt to solve. As we've suggested, attempts to find truth through merely scientific means seem to fall short, because at the end of the day science is incapable of explaining scientifically why science even works. Swinging the pendulum in the opposite direction, however, doesn't seem to leave us any better off. Denying someone their claim to ultimate reality is itself a contrary claim to ultimate reality.

That's where I'd like to start: that universal sense of ought-ness that all of us have, none of us can shake, and no one can seem to explain without God.

"But wait," you say, "couldn't you simply explain our sense of morality through evolution?" And yes, attempts have been made to do just that. Perhaps I'm exaggerating the importance of our inner senses. Maybe what I'm suggesting is an awareness of God's presence and an inability to reason without him isn't really that. Maybe it's a benefit conferred upon us by evolution because at some stage in our development, delusions of God's existence helped us survive as a species. Such a theory of moral origins is certainly popular today, and is widely taught by men like Daniel Dennett. In fact, Dennett wrote a book very much to this effect. To sum up his view he writes:

> *Everything we value—from sugar and sex and money to music and love and religion—we value for reasons. Lying behind, and distinct from, our reasons are evolutionary reasons, free-floating rationales that have been endorsed by natural selection.*[15]

Well there it is, then, right? All our values are simply graced upon us by evolution and endorsed by the machine of natural selection. They aren't telling us what is actually moral, only what we need to believe to help us survive.

But wait. Dennett is suggesting that our belief-forming faculties are not giving us true information about the world around us, they're simply telling us what we need to believe to survive. He's not saying that evolution has given us the power to form correct or true views of the world, he's saying that our beliefs are mere adaptations, totally untethered from what may or may not be true. That's a pretty amazing claim. Responding to such an idea, Tim Keller writes in his book *The Reason for God*:

> *This is a huge Achilles' heel in the whole enterprise of evolutionary biology and theory ... It comes down to this: If, as the evolutionary scientists say, what our brains tell us about morality, love, and beauty is not real – if it is merely a set of chemical reactions designed to pass on our genetic code – then so is what their brains tell them about the world. Then why should we trust them?*[16]

It seems that, again, trying to explain our observations about the world without God, be they scientific or moral, fall apart because they prove too much. We're trying to see through everything, and, as Lewis said, we end up seeing nothing.

---

[15] Quoted in Leon Wieseltier, "The God Genome," *New York Times Book Review*, February 19, 2006.

[16] Tim Keller, *The Reason for God* (New York, NY:Dutton, 2006), 138-9. Alvin Plantinga, also notes, "... there is deep and serious conflict between naturalism and science ... I argue that it is improbable, given naturalism and evolution, that our cognitive faculties are reliable. But then a naturalist who accepts current evolutionary theory has a defeater for the proposition that our faculties are reliable. Furthermore, if she has a defeater for the proposition that her cognitive faculties are reliable, she has a defeater for any belief she takes to be produced by her faculties – including, naturally enough, her belief in naturalism and evolution" *Where the Conflict Really Lies: Science, Religion, and Naturalism* (Oxford, 2011) 18.

What lingering doubts do you have about God?

_____

_____

_____

systematic theology

wayne

REVELATION

I remember once watching a program on television called *Ghost Hunters*. In the show the hunters use various tools – detectors, night-vision goggles, spectrometers, and all sorts of other gadgetry – to search for ghosts. But in the program, you never get to know definitively if they saw a ghost. You just get the best of their speculations. For many, their search for God is similar. They use various tools: meditation, going to church, reading a book – all of it to little avail. So, spirituality in our culture looks a lot like the show I watched – cobbled together speculations based upon hunches, feelings, opinions, and so-called experts. It's as though, to develop our spiritual identity, we all take a walk through the spirituality supermarket, grab a little of this, a handful of that, and check out with our self-contradictory, speculative bag of spiritual groceries.

What if God, instead of expecting us to find him like holy ghost hunters, made himself known to us? What if instead of searching for tiny clues, we adjusted our eyes to see the clues in everything? What if instead of speculation about God, we saw the world around us as revelation from God?

A nearly 500-year-old Christian creed begins by asking the same question: "How do we know God?" The Belgic Confession states:

> *[We know God] first, by the creation, preservation, and government of the universe, since that universe is before our eyes like a beautiful book in which all creatures, great and small, are as letters to make us ponder the invisible things of God ... Second, he makes himself known to us more openly by his holy and divine Word ...*[17]

See, I'm simply repeating ideas from the past that our present culture may have forgotten – the very Christian idea that everything, absolutely everything, has something to say about God. The universe isn't the giant bush that God hides behind, it's the prism through which God radiates his infinitely faceted nature. The hunt isn't a hunt for a God who is hard to find. The hunt is for the best way to understand the clues about him that are all around us.

Further, I'm convinced that you, right where you are, can know him. I echo Lewis' earlier claim that Christianity isn't something I merely see, but the lens through which the world makes the most sense. It's the conclusion that harmonizes the clues all around me. And should we expect any less about God's revelation? If it is indeed from God, then shouldn't it make harmonious what every other view of the world makes dissonant? I certainly think so.

---

[17] The Belgic Confession, Article 2.

Everyone thinks the world reveals *something* – even the most committed atheists. In a recent debate, Richard Dawkins spoke eloquently on what he believes the universe reveals:

> *My interest in the science of biology ... came more from an interest in fundamental questions. I wanted to know why we're all here, what is the meaning of life, why does the universe exist? Why does life exist? That's what drew me to science... I discovered Darwinism [and] recognized there was no good reason to believe in a supernatural creator. I think religious explanations ... are now superseded and outdated. I think that ... all those deep questions that religion once aspired to explain, are now better, more grandly, and in a more beautiful fashion explained by science.*[18]

In short, Dawkins thinks the science of the universe reveals something beyond science ... namely, beauty, grandness, purpose, and the meaning of life. Yet, his own worldview precludes such "beyond science" phenomena from actually existing at all.

Here we find a strange area of agreement between myself and the distinguished Professor Dawkins. We both believe that the universe holds answers to major questions. We both agree that all around us are clues to our ultimate meaning, origins, purpose, and destiny. What's curious is that he thinks that science is somehow able to deliver definitive answers to questions of purpose, meaning, and destiny. I'm curious to know what experiment a biologist can perform to deduce destiny. What microbial behaviors do we observe to find meaning? Strange, isn't it? It all sounds terribly unscientific for a man like him. And it sounds that way because it is.

What drove Dawkins into science are, ironically, the very questions that science is incapable of answering. It would be a bit like using a metal detector to find happiness. Metal detectors detect metal not happiness. It's not that happiness isn't there – it's just not detectable by the metal detector. Science is simply the wrong tool, or at least, it's the wrong tool all by itself.

Can science alone tell us the meaning of life, of love, of beauty, good, and evil? The fact that the universe exploded into existence 13.6 billion years ago in an unimaginably powerful and bright explosion of space, time, matter, and energy tells me how (we think, at least) this all got started. It does not tell me why, or for what purpose. Nor can it.

It seems to me that if questions about the meaning of life, truth, beauty, and goodness are themselves outside of the natural realm in their scope, then the answers must come from a similar location ... outside nature. If I sound naive, then I'm at least in good company. Great minds have struggled with this question since philosophy and reason showed up on the landscape of human thought. How can we grasp ultimate reality? What's beyond this world? These are the questions that have preoccupied the deeper thinkers among us for millennia. The discipline of philosophy has pitched and rolled between varying attempts to answer such questions.

If the search for ultimate reality – for God – is really about simply stacking speculation upon speculation, no matter how solid those speculations may be, then just skip it. Seriously. It's a failed journey from the start. God, by definition, is limitless in power, scope, depth, and a host of other aspects. If knowing God is simply about stacking up my speculations then we're as silly for doing that as our ancestors were in attempting the Tower of Babel. We still do this – build our own towers, but our supplies aren't bricks and mortar, they're speculations and musings. Stacking them ever so well, we hope that at some point we'll hit God, or ultimate reality, or whatever else we'd like to call it. But how can we actually ascend that high?

---

[18] Richard Dawkins, The God Delusion Debate, hosted by Fixed Point Foundation. Birmingham, AL, 2006.

Cue revelation. The word literally means "to pull back the veil." So, what God does in revealing himself to us is to pull back the veil of his infinity enough for us to see some of who he is. We don't ascend to him, he descends to us. We don't search for him, he shows himself to us. Revelation is all around us, because everything around us, if it was made by God, would rather sensibly bear his mark.[19]

For example, we can look at the human genome and see the most complex, information-rich language known to exist.[20] We could therefore, assume that God is intelligent. Or, we might look at the beauty of creation and rightly conclude that God must be beautiful and creative. Perhaps we peer through a telescope at the seemingly limitless cosmos and imagine, "God must be very, very strong." These aren't strange conclusions to draw considering the world around us. They are, ironically, perfectly natural.

Read Romans 1:19-20. What does this text teach us about a general knowledge of God?

DITCHES

Jesus described the road to knowing God as narrow, only being found by a few.[21] As I stated earlier, my goal is for you to know God. I mean really know him – as a person knows a friend. But if we're going to venture down that road, then we'd better pay attention to the warning Jesus would give to all who would seek: watch out that you don't fall off the road.

On one side is the ditch of *Modernism*, which is a school of thought that heavily emphasizes rationality, proof, and logic. It would be possible for us to be so distracted by the complex beauty of philosophy and theology that we get entirely distracted from knowing God – which is the goal of those disciplines. Put simply, knowing *about* God is not the same as knowing God. God, if he is there at all, must be more than just an idea, he must be personal. It's logically incoherent to imagine that personhood simply arrived out of the curious arrangement of atoms over millions of years. Personhood must come from a

---

[19] Let me say at this point that the main goal of this book isn't to outline all the possible lines of argument for God's existence. That would be a very long book, and there have been many good books written to this effect. The approach that I'm taking is something often called the transcendental argument for God's existence. That is to say, I'm attempting to briefly illustrate that without God, the universe, life, meaning, logic, and a host of other things become inexplicable. There are other lines of reasoning, and for some of them I might suggest William Lane Craig's *A Reasonable Faith* and Tim Keller's *The Reason for God* as good places to start.

[20] For a very helpful discussion on the topic of the human genome as a language which is the product of a divine mind, see Stephen C. Meyer, *Signature in the Cell*. (New York, NY: Harper Collins, 2009).

[21] Matthew 7:13-14

person. The mistake of Modernism is to reduce God to a long bullet-pointed list of propositions, forgetting that God is personal.

Of course, we can't do that with each other. If you hand me a sheet of paper with 25 true statements about you, I can hardly say I know you. Persons aren't simply known by facts about them, but experience with them. Our aim, therefore, must be to know more than just facts. If facts were the big deal, then the people who knew God the most would be the smartest among us. Where would that leave the rest of us? Facts are important, but if we start to think that memorizing a set of statements about God means that we know him, then we'd quickly find ourselves in a ditch. We may know a lot about God, but not really know him.

On the other side is the ditch of *Postmodernism*. Part of this framework is the belief that truth isn't to be found in mere statements of fact. Truth is communal, living, and personal. It's entirely possible to approach the project of knowing God in this way, untethering ourselves from anything that looks like a creed. If modernism is all about the facts, then postmodernism is all about the feels. But of course, this doesn't work either. Again, if God is a person, then after knowing him you won't be able to not know facts about him. If you're married and you don't know the fact of the date of your anniversary, then you've got troubles, my friend. Why? Because the best kind of knowing involves both personal experience and factual understanding. If you ever start to doubt that, go ahead and forget your anniversary. See how that works out for you.

Which of these two "ditches" do you naturally tend toward? How will you avoid the ditches?
_____
_____
_____

A WAY FORWARD

Imagine if I were to hire a team of the best psychiatrists and psychoanalysts in the world with one job: write for me the most detailed list of factual observations about my wife. Months later, they hand me volumes of research and data that they've collected from their hard work. Then imagine that I start to study, and commit those observations to perfect memory. Would I know my wife? Of course not. Knowing my wife involves far more than simply knowing correct information about her. It requires relationship with her. In the end, it may turn out that I have a command of every one of those facts that my topnotch team of psychologists assembled, but it's more than mere academic knowledge. Knowing persons means knowing right facts about them as well as having experiences with them. It's knowledge coupled with experience. It's life *and* doctrine.

God is a person who wishes to relate to us. As it turns out, it's creeds *and* feelings, experience *and* exhaustive study.

J.I. Packer, a great and wise Christian theologian and professor warns us well when he writes ...

> *We need to ask ourselves: what is my ultimate aim and object in occupying my mind with these things? What do I intend to do with my knowledge about God, once I have got it? For the fact that we have to face is this: that if we pursue theological knowledge for its own sake, it is bound to go bad on us. It will make us proud and conceited. The very greatness of the subject matter will intoxicate us, and we shall come to think of ourselves as a cut above other Christians because of our interest in it ... Our aim in studying God must be to know God himself ...[22]*

The goal is to know God; God, the person. Given what we've said here, an important question comes up. How? How are we to know him? It's that question to which our attention now turns.

Read Jeremiah 9:23-24. What are we to "glory in?" What does that mean for you?

_____
_____
_____

[Handwritten notes:]
2: Bibliology
3: Theology
4: Creation
5: The Fall
6: Since the fall
7: What it means to be a christian
8:
9: The study of the end times

---

[22] J.I. Packer. *Knowing God.* (InterVarsity Press, 1993) 20-21.

Knowing – **Chapter One**

APPLICATION & REFLECTION

1. Read Matthew 11:27. According to this verse, who knows God? What does it take to know God?

2. According to 1 Corinthians 1:21, can we know God through worldly wisdom and speculation?

3. Do you want to know God? Why? Read John 17:3

4. What is General Revelation? What is Special Revelation? What's the difference? How does *The Belgic Confession* explain the relationship between nature and scripture?

5. How are faith and science related, according to *The Belgic Concession*?

6. Read Psalm 84:1-5. How did David feel about knowing God? How do you feel about knowing God?

7. What did you learn in this lesson and how will you apply it to your life?

_____
_____
_____

SCRIPTURE

John 17:3	Philippians 3:10	Psalm 84:1-5
Ecclesiastes 3:10	Jeremiah 9:23-24	
Psalm 119:105	Matthew 11:27	Psalm 19:1-2

CHAPTER TWO

WORDS

Chapter Two – Words

DON'T GET TOO SPECIFIC, GOD

In the previous chapter, I wanted to show that God can be known if (and only if) God reveals himself. So, this is where we might stop and say, "Okay, God has revealed himself in a general way. We can assume he's there, he's powerful, and a few other things." But go much beyond that level of specificity and we become uncomfortable. We are quite happy with a God who is there, but vague. Why? Because if God is vague then we can claim ignorance. And in our happy ignorance we may begin to feel like we've got a good excuse for our behavior, just in case anyone should ask. After all, we didn't really know God specifically wanted us to not do that, right?

In fact, vague spirituality is the religion *du jour*. We prefer the fogginess of our opinions about God over any kind of definitive revelation from God. In a recent study of American spirituality, Christian Smith coined a term to describe what his research found to be the rising trend: "moralistic therapeutic deism."[23] That is, a spirituality that gives us moral guidance vaguely, personal help therapeutically, but doesn't tell us anything authoritatively.

Such a version of religion is not the message of any scripture nor the dogma of any creed, but the preference of the Western mind. Give me the kind of god who makes me act nice, feel nice, and please leave the rest to me, thank you very much. We're comfortable with God, out there … somewhere. We just don't want to be too specific, because then we can live however we want.

Read Psalm 119:97-98. What was David's attitude toward the Scriptures? What is yours?
___
___
___

IS IT WRONG TO CALL IT "GOD'S WORD?"

In a pluralistic culture like ours, it's hardly surprising that many reject the notion that anyone really knows God, much less have his actual words in a book somewhere. While this objection is understandable and emotionally poignant, it has problems. The one making the claim "no one should say they have God's word," is speaking a kind of divine word. The claim is self-refuting.

Yet, everyone already acts as though certain truths are objective, ultimate, and universally binding on all people. For the atheistic naturalist, ultimate truth lies in the objective power of science to answer all our questions. For the Marxist utopian, the

---

[23] Christian Smith and Melina Ludquist Denton. *Soul Searching: The Religious and Spiritual Lives of American Teenagers.* (New York, NY: Oxford University Press), 2005.

ultimate truth lies in the eternal struggle of the underclasses to achieve revolution, which will bring about communal humanity. The same goes for the feminist, the jihadist, the pantheist, and everyone of every other worldview. Thus, the question can't be whether it's right to say you have ultimate truth (or, God's words, in this case). The real question must be, which "truth" is true?

> **Read Psalm 1:1-3. Describe the person who meditates on Scripture.**
>
> _____
> _____
> _____

WHAT IS THE BIBLE?

The Bible claims to be God's special revelation to humanity, which roots its authority on the life, death, and subsequent resurrection of Jesus Christ. It is a book of books which contain the story of God, and how he made us and wishes to relate to us. Along with what can be known about ultimate reality through the natural world (general revelation), God has uniquely revealed himself through his written word (the Bible) and his incarnate Word (Jesus Christ).

First, a definition. The Bible is a book of books, sixty-six of them, in fact. This book of books is divided into two sections – the Old Testament and the New Testament – all of which come together to form what we call today the Bible.

The Bible includes many different genres of writing, including history, sermons, letters, songs, poems, architectural plans, family trees, and various other forms. It was completed over a span of 1,500 years (over 40 generations), and was written by over 40 human authors from every background (kings, peasants, philosophers, fishermen, poets, scholars, etc.)[24] It was written in three languages (Hebrew, Aramaic, and Greek), making it not the product of any one generation, guru, people, ethnicity, or culture. In short, the Christian Scriptures are multiethnic, multicultural, and global.

Repeatedly, the bible claims to contain God's words. The phrase, "Thus says the Lord" shows up around 415 times from cover to cover. Just by sheer weight, the claim to God's speech is impressive. The Apostle Paul makes the argument even more forcefully, writing,

> *All Scripture is breathed out by God and profitable for teaching, for reproof, for correction and for training in righteousness.*
> (2 Timothy 3:16).

That little phrase "breathed out by God" is very important. There is a deep and mystical claim here: the Bible is more than words on a page, but comes from His Spirit as his eternal, immutable words. Peter agrees with Paul, saying,

---

[24] Mark Driscoll, *The Gospel Class Manual* (Seattle, WA: Mars Hill)

Chapter Two – Words

> *... no prophecy of Scripture comes from someone's own interpretation. For no prophecy was ever produced by the will of man, but men spoke from God as they were carried along by the Holy Spirit. (2 Peter 1:20-21).*

Famous Bible scholar B.B. Warfield agrees, saying,

> *It goes beyond all such terms [as "guidance"] ... What is borne [or carried along] is taken up by the bearer, The Holy Spirit, and conveyed by the bearer's power, not his own, to the bearer's goal, not his own. The men who spoke for The Holy Spirit are here declared, therefore, to have been taken up by the Holy Spirit and brought by his power to the goal of his choosing. The things which they spoke under the operation of the Spirit were therefore his things, not theirs.*[25]

That obviously doesn't prove that the Bible is actually God's word, but it's important that we at least start out understanding that it claims that it is. This keeps us from being able to say that it's merely a nice, helpful book with some good stories. A book that claims to be God's words is either (a) God's words, or (b) not God's words. If it is (a) then we should pay close attention to what it says. If it's not God's words but merely claiming to be (b), then it's a book with some serious lies in it, in which case, it really isn't a good book to live by, and we should probably discard it.

I can claim to be a fish, but that doesn't mean I can breathe underwater. If we're going to move the Bible's claim forward, we need more. And more is just what we have. Much more. Here's what Sydney Collet has to say about the Bible.

In his recent book *Can We Still Believe the Bible,* Craig Blomberg examines many of the doubts modern people express related to the Bible and concludes,

> *[T]hese Scriptures are trustworthy. We can still believe the Bible. We should still believe the Bible, and act accordingly ...* [26]

This is pretty hefty claim. Let's see if we can support it.

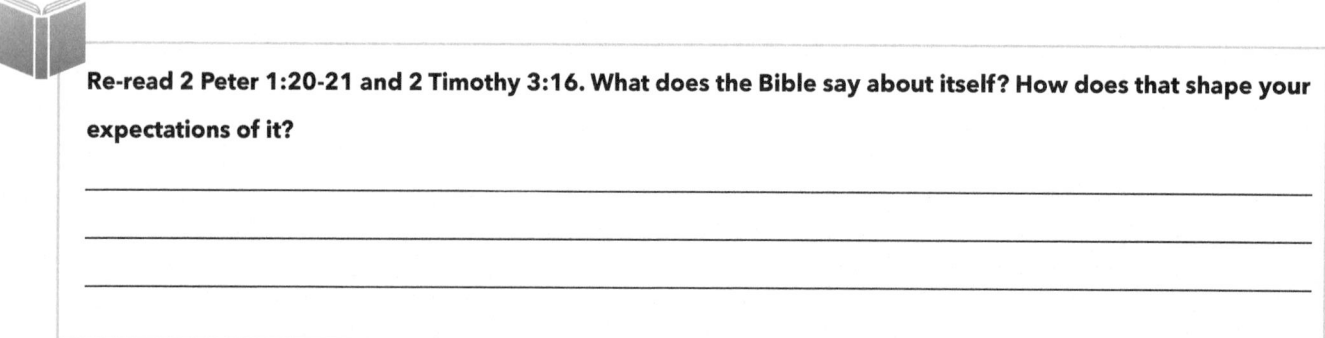

Re-read 2 Peter 1:20-21 and 2 Timothy 3:16. What does the Bible say about itself? How does that shape your expectations of it?

_____
_____
_____

---

[25] B.B. Warfeild, *The Biblical Idea of Inspiration* from *The Works of BB Warfeild.* (Baker House Books, 1978)

[26] Blomberg, Craig (2014-04-01). *Can We Still Believe the Bible?: An Evangelical Engagement with Contemporary Questions* (Kindle Locations 4532-4533). Baker Publishing Group. Kindle Edition.

ISN'T THE BIBLE FULL OF MISTAKES?

In the book *Misquoting Jesus*, popular New Testament scholar Bart Ehrman lays out the reasons that we shouldn't trust the Bible. As a former evangelical, his claims smack the reader rather poignantly. He says,

> *As we learned at Moody [Bible Institute] in one of the first courses in the curriculum, we don't actually have the original writings of the New Testament. What we have are copies of these writings, made years later – in most cases, many years later. Moreover, none of these copies is completely accurate, since the scribes who produced them inadvertently and/or intentionally changed them in places.*[27]

Sounds like a powerful argument, doesn't it? The case seems to only be made more sure when Ehrman explains that the New Testament manuscripts available to Scholars today have over 200,000 inconsistencies between them.[28] With numbers like that, how can we be sure that the Bible is anything like what Mark, James, or any other biblical author actually wrote?

The answer to these objections is far less dramatic than their presentation, I'm afraid. Please allow me to quote a review of Ehrman's position here:

> *Ehrman clearly wants the reader to believe that the increase in available manuscript evidence has increased the scope of the problem. But before accepting that this is true based on Ehrman's clever presentation, take a few moments to do some math with me. I think you will find, as I did, that what Bart Ehrman has created for the reader is a verbal and numerical illusion ... The fact is, Ehrman included this arbitrary and irrelevant comparison in order to stun the reader with an ultimately useless bit of information.... if all the manuscripts were complete, that would be somewhere in excess of 2.2 billion words. Since many of the manuscripts are partial, however, the number is probably closer to one billion. ... Most importantly (as Ehrman finally admits in the last chapter), "of all the hundreds of thousands of textual changes found among our manuscripts, most of them are completely insignificant, immaterial, of no real importance for anything other than showing that scribes could not spell or keep focused any better than the rest of us" (p. 207). The fact [is] that the vast majority of these textual variants are "completely insignificant, immaterial, of no real importance for anything ... " After taking the time and effort to put all of this together ... I was left wondering what all the fuss was about in the first place.*[29]

Have you ever played the game called "telephone?" Here's how it goes: I whisper something to Susie who whispers it to Johnny. Johnny whispers it to Sam, and Sam whispers it to Philip, etc., until it gets back to me. As you may suspect, by the time it gets back to me, it's hardly recognizable as having anything to do with what I originally told Susie.

I remember as a freshman in college attending my first Intro to Religion class and being told that the transmission of the New Testament documents was essentially like a 2,000-year-long game of telephone. If that was the case, how could we really trust

---

[27] Bart Ehrman, *Misquoting Jesus*. (New York, NY: HarperCollins, 2005), 5.

[28] Ibid, 89-90.

[29] Wingerd, Daryl. "Bart Ehrman's Misquoting Jesus - A Critical Review." Christian Communicators Worldwide, 2006, http://www.ccwtoday.org/article_view.asp?

Chapter Two – Words

the Bible as God's word to us? As a freshman in college, I must confess I was dumbstruck at the comparison and had no way to respond. I left the class discouraged, wondering if I, as a Christian, had built my life on documents that weren't anything like what the biblical authors had written.

Upon returning to my dorm room, my confusion gave way to curiosity. I began exploring the topic that my professor had brought up. I searched through books on what I found out was called the field of textual criticism, and found out that my professor was, simply stated, wrong. The writings in your Bible are not the inventions of scribes locked in a monastery during the dark ages, concocted to consolidate the power of the church. They turn out to be extraordinarily trustworthy copies of what the original authors wrote. The Bible is not, in fact, full of copyist errors and political agendas, selectively imposed to make the church look good. The following table illustrates the overwhelming point that the documents of the New Testament are present in far greater number from antiquity, with far greater reliability, than any other source documents that we've ever come across.

AUTHOR	DATE WRITTEN	EARLIEST COPY	TIME SPAN	NUMBER OF COPIES	ACCURACY BETWEEN COPIES
PLATO	427-347 BC	900 AD	1200 YRS	7	---
HERODITUS	480-425 BC	900 AD	1300 YRS	8	---
THUCYDIDES	460-400 BC	900 AD	1300 YRS	8	---
EURIPIDES	480-406 BC	1100 AD	1300 YRS	9	---
ARISTOPHANES	450-395 BC	900 AD	1200 YRS	10	---
CAESER	100-44 BC	900 AD	1000 YRS	10	---
TACITUS	CIRCA 100 AD	1100 AD	1000 YRS	20	---
ARISTOTLE	384-322 BC	1100 AD	1400 YRS	49	---
HOMER (ILLIAD)	900 BC	400 BC	500 YRS	643	95%
NEW TESTAMENT	50-90 AD	120 AD	LESS THAN 100 YRS	5600+	99.5%

[30]

The New Testament documents stack up rather well against other ancient documents. We simply have exponentially more of them, from more sources, closer to the actual dates of the events, with far greater accuracy between them, than we do for any other ancient historical document.

Furthermore, claiming we can't really know what the original authors wrote proves too much. To say that the New Testament documents aren't reliable representations of what the original authors intended is to simultaneously call into question everything we take for granted about ancient history from every other ancient document. In other words, if you throw out the New Testament for this reason, then you also throw out the ability to know almost anything from any other ancient document. Of the few variations that do exist within the ancient manuscripts, virtually all yield to vigorous textual criticism. This means that

---

[30] The Chart above has been synthesized from Ken Boa's *I'm Glad You Asked*, Norman Geisler's *Christian Apologetics*, Josh Mcdowel's *A Ready Defense*, and Richard M. Fales' article "Archaeology and History Attest to the Bible," in The Evidence Bible (Bridge-Logos, 2001).

our New Testament is around 99.5% textually pure. Together, we find that the variants within are so small and insignificant that they in no way have an impact on the message of the Scriptures concerning how we as human beings relate to God.[31]

> *The Christian has substantially superior criteria for affirming the New Testament documents than he does for any other ancient writing. It is good evidence on which to base the trust in the reliability of the New Testament.*[32]

What are some of the problem with saying that the Bible we have isn't reliable?

_____
_____
_____

ISN'T THE BIBLE CULTURALLY BACKWARDS?

Many who object to the "revelation" status of the Bible do so on different grounds – they find its message offensive and culturally backwards. In a recent sermon at Cambridge University, the objection was raised this way:

> *[Hasn't the Bible] passed its sell by date? Is it increasingly obsolete? Many believe so. It has its merits, people say, much that is spiritually inspiring but to see it as authoritative? To see it as God's revealed and unchanging word? How could you possibly think that when so much of it is outmoded; so many of its ideas primitive and culturally regressive? Take its views on slavery and women for a start. They alone are enough to show that we have moved on and that the Bible belongs to a bygone age. Which is why many want to pick and choose; there are parts I like and parts I don't like; parts I profit from and parts I find frankly embarrassing.*[33]

My wife is originally from a very small town in Louisiana. In this particular town, there is still a very strong cultural memory of the racism that fueled segregation. What was so crazy about those times was how seemingly good, moral people had convinced themselves that the systematic oppression of a people based on skin color was good and right. On a recent visit back to the small town of her early childhood, we wondered what we might be doing today that in fifty years our grandchildren would find unbelievably wrong.

---

[31] Geisler, Norman L., Nix, William E., *A General Introduction to the Bible* (Chicago: Moody Press, 1986), 475.

[32] Norman Geisler & Peter Bocchino, *Unshakeable Foundations* (Minneapolis, MN: Bethany House Publishers, 2001) 256.

[33] Steve Midgley, "Is the Bible Culturally Irrelevant?" (sermon, Jesus College, Cambridge University, Cambridge, UK, November 13, 2011), http://www.jesus.cam.ac.uk/chapel-choir/chapel-services/sermons/is-the-bible-culturally-irrelevant/ (accessed September 6, 2012).

Chapter Two – Words

I share this to illustrate a point: to say that the Bible is culturally backwards you have to believe that we have collectively arrived at the pinnacle of cultural development. It takes quite a bit of cultural and chronological arrogance to think that the wisdom of today is wiser than the wisdom of the past. And what's more troubling, it's nearly impossible to guess with accuracy what our culture will say is good in another hundred years. And even if we could know what they'd say, who's to say they'd be right?

To judge the Scriptures as being culturally backwards, one must be convinced of one's own culture's ascendancy to universal greatness. But think about that for a moment. The last time you read the news, were you not immediately reminded of your culture's problems and failings? The last time you voted, was it not to improve your culture, hoping this candidate would solve the problems that vex our society? Doesn't that mean that the plumb line you're judging the Bible against is a bit skewed?

Suppose for a moment the Bible isn't a backwards book of old-time conventions, but God's revealed word to all cultures and times. Additionally, suppose that the God who sent these words was a God outside of time and above all cultures. If those thoughts are true, wouldn't we expect something in these words to run upstream to our culture? At some point, shouldn't it critique every culture? It turns out that critiquing the culture isn't a reason to reject the Bible at all. For, if it really is God's word, then this is exactly what we might expect it to do.

Keller expands on this idea:

> Many of us read a certain passage of scripture and say, "That's so regressive, so offensive." But we ought to entertain the idea that maybe we feel that way because in our particular culture that text is a problem. In other cultures that passage might not come across as regressive or offensive.
>
> Let's look at just one example. In individualistic, Western societies, we read the Bible, and we have a problem with what it says about sex. But then we read what the Bible says about forgiveness ... we say, "How wonderful!" It's because we are driven by a culture of guilt. But if you were to go to the Middle East, they would think that what the Bible has to say about sex is pretty good. (Actually, they might feel it's not strict enough!) But when they would read what the Bible says about forgiving your enemies, it would strike them as absolutely crazy. It's because their culture is not an individualistic society like ours. It's more of a shame culture than a guilt culture.
>
> Let me ask you a question: If you're offended by something in the Bible, why should your cultural sensibilities trump everybody else's? Why should we get rid of the Bible because it offends your culture? Let's do a thought experiment for a second. If the Bible really was the revelation of God, and therefore it wasn't the product of any one culture, wouldn't it contradict every culture at some point? Therefore if it's really from God, wouldn't it have to offend your cultural sensibilities at some point? Therefore when you read the Bible, and you find some part of it outrageous and offensive, that's proof that it's probably true, that it's probably from God. It's not a reason to say the Bible isn't God's Word; it's a reason to say it is. What makes you think that because this part or that part of God's Word is offensive, you can forget Christianity altogether?[34]

---

[34] Tim Keller, "Literalism: Isn't the Bible Historically Unreliable and Regressive?" (sermon, Redeemer Presbyterian Church, New York, NY, 2009), http:www.preachingtoday.com%2Ffiles%2Fpt%2Fsermons%2Ftranscript%2Fpt846.pdf&ei=POVIUMKfNIfc0QH7-4HYBQ&usg=AFQj (accessed September 6, 2012).

We must at least be open to the possibility that the Bible can contradict us, even on matters close to our hearts. Why? Well, contradiction is a function of relationship. If God is really there, really personal, and really knowable, then we'd expect him to contradict us from time to time, wouldn't we?

> **What parts of Scripture do you find culturally out of step? Based on what you've read, how might you move forward with those questions and doubts?**
>
> _____
> _____
> _____

COULDN'T THE BIBLE JUST BE A MYTH?

In the same Intro to Religion class I mentioned earlier, I was assigned to read two other works of ancient near east literature, the *Bhagavad Gita* and *Enuma Elish*. The point of the assignment was to illustrate to the class how other ancient myths were similar to the Bible, and how therefore the Bible was likely mythological as well.

I must confess, I didn't like this assignment at all. It wasn't because I had to read the other books – I like to read. It was that after reading them, I couldn't for the life of me see how they were at all like anything I'd ever read anywhere in the Scriptures. Despite my inability to see where my professor was coming from, he was insistent, and to my amazement others among my class were nodding their heads in dutiful agreement. Was I missing something?

Back to the dorm room, and back to reading more books to understand what I was being taught. As it turned out, I found one very powerful scholar who had a similar problem to me. He also thought that the Bible was unique as a piece of literature and not like the ancient myths of the past. His name was C.S. Lewis.

Lewis noted two powerful lines of reasoning against calling the Bible a simple collection of meaningless, non-historical mythologies. First is the fact that the documents which make up the Bible simply do not bear resemblance to any ancient mythologies. You know the old phrase, "If it waddles like a duck and quacks like a duck, then it's probably a duck." Well, in this case, there is neither waddling nor quacking.

Quite the opposite, actually, is what we find in the pages of the Scriptures. Instead, they claim to be accurate reporting of actual historical events:

Chapter Two – Words

> *Inasmuch as many have undertaken to compile a narrative of the things that have been accomplished among us, just as those who from the beginning were eyewitnesses and ministers of the word have delivered them to us, it seemed good to me also, having followed all things closely for some time past, to write an orderly account for you, most excellent Theophilus ... (Luke 1:1-3)*
>
> *For we did not follow cleverly devised myths when we made known to you the power and coming of our Lord Jesus Christ, but we were eyewitnesses of his majesty. (2 Peter 1:16)*
>
> *... that which we have seen and heard we proclaim also to you, so that you too may have fellowship with us; and indeed our fellowship is with the Father and with his Son Jesus Christ. (1 John 1:3)*

Add to all of this one more line of thought. Imagine you were a third-century Christian scribe, and your job was to doctor up the Bible, would you include in your edition narrative passages that make your leaders look like buffoons? Throughout the pages of the New Testament we see the disciples making mistakes, missing what Jesus was trying to teach them, or acting cowardly. How would the inclusion of that information be at all beneficial in the eyes of a power-hungry scribe? Further, why would such scribes include passages which tell of women being the first eyewitness of Jesus' resurrection unless it really happened? In that day, the testimony of a woman wasn't even admissible in court. What good would it have done your cause to add in such seemingly counterproductive information? Answer: no good at all.

That is, unless you weren't editing, but copying.

The presence of this counterproductive narrative, as it has been called, is very strong evidence for the fact that the document in question is not mythology, but ancient eyewitness accounts of what actually took place in the eyes of the authors. C.S. Lewis sums up the point nicely when he says,

> *I have been reading poems, romances, vision-literature, legends, myths all my life. I know what they are like. I know that not one [of the stories in the Gospel of John, for example] is like this... Either this is reportage - Or else, some unknown writer in the second century, without known predecessors or successors, suddenly anticipated the whole technique of modern, novelistic, realistic narrative...*[35]

So, let's put to rest this idea that the Bible was written as a mythology.

Review the Scriptures above. What does the Bible seem to be saying about itself? How does that inform your reading of it?

_____

_____

_____

---

[35] C.S. Lewis, "Modern Theology and Biblical Criticism," *Christian Reflections* (Eerdmans, 1967)

IS THE BIBLE HISTORICALLY ACCURATE?

Archaeology and ancient history have repeatedly borne out the claims of the Bible. Ancient historians such as Josephus, Pliny the Younger, Tacitus, Lucian, and the Jewish Talmud all attest to different instances of the Christian Scriptures accurately representing the history it details. The more we dig, the more we find evidence to support, not contradict the claims of the Scriptures.

> *There exists no document from the ancient world witnessed by so excellent a set of textual and historical testimonies and offering so superb an array of historical data on which an intelligent decision may be made. An honest [person] cannot dismiss a source of this kind. Skepticism regarding the historical credentials of Christianity is based upon an irrational bias.*[36]

When we examine the Scriptures for their historicity, the remarkable observation that we walk away with is not their unbelievability. What we should note is that for thousands of years, no one has been able to disprove the historicity of the 66 books of the Old and New Testaments. That can't be said of other so-called religious documents.[37]

In fact, what we find within the pages of this book seem, rather sonorously, to sing the same song.

THE NOTES SEEM TO HARMONIZE

Imagine that I told you there was a symphony which was written by forty or so different composers over a millennia or two. What might such a piece of music sound like? Likely, the whole thing should be expected to sound like an odd, confusing mess.

The Bible is different. Here we find a book of books with a unified message — like movements of a symphony all written around a single motif. Such unity is remarkable. What we have in the Bible is one book of books which all point to one, overarching story — namely, the story of God's rescuing, holy, redeeming love, which culminates in the life, death, and resurrection of Jesus Christ.

Like a golden thread woven through a tapestry of deep dark hues and playful bright colors, the whole narrative thrust of the Bible from beginning to end centers on the revelation of God in Jesus Christ. Narratives hinge on Jesus. Prophecies written hundreds of years beforehand come to pass in Jesus. Songs anticipate Jesus. Poetry extols the coming of Jesus. So harmonious is the whole that we can trace Jesus through each of the parts:

---

[36] Clark Pinnock, *Set Forth Your Case*. (New Jersey: The Craig Press, 1968) 58.

[37] For example, about The Book of Mormon, The National Geographic Society, in a 1998 letter to the Institute for Religious Research, stated "Archaeologists and other scholars have long probed the hemisphere's past and the society does not know of anything found so far that has substantiated the Book of Mormon." The Qu'ran is also noted to contain serious historical errors, including the claim that Jesus wasn't crucified — this is a claim that all extra-biblical evidence contradicts.

Chapter Two – Words

- He shows up at the Word present at creation (Gen. 1:2).
- He is prophesied to be born of a woman (Gen. 3:15),
- He is a descendant of Abraham (Gen. 22:18 cf. Matt 1:1)
- He is born in Bethlehem (Mic. 5:2 cf. Luke 2)
- He would be anticipated by a forerunner, John the Baptist (Is. 40; Mal. 3:1 cf. John 1:19-52).
- Hundreds of years before he ever shows up we're told that Jesus would be rejected by his own people (Is. 53),
- He would be betrayed by a close friend for thirty pieces of silver (Ps. 41:9 cf. Matt. 26:50, Zech. 11:2),
- The blood money would be thrown on the floor of the temple, which was destroyed in 70 A.D., meaning that the prophesied Messiah had to have come before then (Zech. 11:13 cf. Matt. 27:5-7).
- His crucifixion next to thieves was foretold (Ps. 22:16, Is. 53:12 cf. Matt. 27:38),
- His resurrection is foretold (Ps. 16:10, Isa. 52:13, 53:10-12 cf. Acts 2:25-32).

If this were a piece of music, the motif would be clear and the notes would be harmonizing beautifully. Summarizing the point, Blomberg writes:

> ... it is hard to take entire documents from antiquity of the same literary genre as any given book in the Protestant canon of Old and New Testaments, read them straight through from beginning to end, and claim they have as many marks of being as "God-breathed" (theopneustos, the quality Paul predicates of Scripture in 2 Tim. 3: 16) as the sixty-six books spanning Genesis to Revelation. Particularly significant is the way any such addition would interrupt, to one degree or another, the tightly knit unity within the diversity of the Jewish and Christian canons. No other books, moreover, read as if the authors might be consciously supplementing Scripture, naturally carrying on its story line, and building on its authoritative foundation without ever ... contradicting it.[38]

Who is the central figure of the story of the Bible? How should that change how we read it?

_____
_____
_____

---

[38] Blomberg, Craig (2014-04-01). Can We Still Believe the Bible?: An Evangelical Engagement with Contemporary Questions (Kindle Locations 1414-1418). Baker Publishing Group. Kindle Edition.

THE NAILS UPON WHICH THE MATTER HANGS

Knowing God requires Him to reveal himself. While the world God made certainly speaks volumes about him, something more is needed. He's got to speak about himself – and that's exactly what the Bible claims to be; the spoken word of God, from God, about God, for us.

It's historical. It's not mythical. It's consistent, not contradictory. It's supra-cultural, not culturally regressive. All of this seems to be clear from the Scriptures themselves. And yet, there's one matter more which grounds the Scriptures as trustworthy testimony: what they say about Jesus Christ. The fact is, if Jesus Christ rose from the dead, then we can trust the Bible. If he did not, then we cannot.

The good news is that the resurrection of Jesus Christ from the dead is a rather strongly attested to fact of history. For the sake of brevity, let us consider three good reasons to trust the historical record related to this event. First, it is a fact that the tomb in which Jesus was placed was empty three days later. Jacob Kremer, an Austrian scholar who has specialized in the study of the resurrection, says, "by far most scholars hold firmly to the reliability of the biblical statements about the empty tomb."[39] Furthermore, it must also be taken as history that Jesus' disciples such as Peter had experiences in which Jesus appeared to them as the Christ.[40] In fact, many of these post-resurrection appearances were witnessed not only by believers but by unbelievers, skeptics, and even enemies.[41] And finally, the early disciples came, rather suddenly, to believe that Jesus Christ had risen from the dead, despite having every predisposition not to.[42]

That third point should be expanded upon. The early disciples were first-century Palestinian Jews under Roman occupation. The kind of Messiah that everyone was hoping for was not the one Jesus turned out to be. Jews at that time were expecting their Messiah to come and kick out the Romans and reestablish the Jewish nation-state to its former glory. There was no expectation of a dying and rising deliverer. Yet, the disciples, who were culturally and religiously conditioned not to believe that Messiah would die and rise again, did. They believed this fact so strongly that they ended up giving their very lives for that belief. All this of course begs the question, "Why would they do that?"

Clearly, some sort of very powerful, transformative experience took place in the lives of each one of these men.[43] Did they all decide to lie about their dead Messiah? Perhaps, but it seems hardly worth it to give your life up for a lie. Was Jesus' body stolen? Again, it's possible but unlikely as there is no historical evidence to support such a claim. So, what are we left with to explain the facts? Resurrection. That's it. That's the only experience surprising, powerful, and transformational enough to explain all the evidence. That's why imminent historian N.T. Wright says, "as an historian, I cannot explain the rise of early Christianity unless Jesus rose again, leaving an empty tomb behind him."[44]

---

[39] Jacob Kremer, *Die Osterevangelien--Geschichten um Geschichte* (Stuttgart: Katholisches Bibelwerk, 1977), pp. 49-50.

[40] Gerd Lüdemann, *What Really Happened to Jesus?*, trans. John Bowden (Louisville, Kent.: Westminster John Knox Press, 1995), p. 8.

[41] Craig, William Lane. "Does God Exist?" Reasonable Faith. http://www.reasonablefaith.org/does-god-exist-1 (accessed September 12, 2012).

[42] For a fuller treatment of the history and historicity of the resurrection, see N.T. Wright, *The Resurrection of the Son of God*.

[43] Luke Timothy Johnson, *The Real Jesus* (San Francisco: Harper San Francisco, 1996), p. 136.

[44] N. T. Wright, "The New Unimproved Jesus," Christianity Today (September 13, 1993), p. 26.

Chapter Two – Words

BETTER THAN SPECULATION

Christians believe the Bible is Special Revelation. Thinking through how the Bible has come to us, it's easier to see why. Preserved over millennia, authored by a diverse collection of men from all walks of life, written across continents, and yet delivering one unified message far greater than the sum of its parts. The testimony contained within the Scriptures appears, by all accounts, to be trustworthy. No other religious book even comes close to such rigorous historical inquiry and remains standing like your very own Bible does. And that fact leads us to another question.

Just what kind of God does your Bible reveal?

Words – **Chapter Two**

APPLICATION & REFLECTION

1. Before reading this, what were some misconceptions you had about the Bible? What did you learn in this chapter that helped you understand what the Bible actually is?

   _____
   _____
   _____

2. According to Hebrews 4:12, what is the word of God like?

   _____
   _____

3. Read Psalm 119:97-104. What were the Psalmist's feelings about the word of God?

   _____
   _____

4. Read Joshua 1:8. What did God promise to Joshua? What must Joshua do?

   _____
   _____

5. What is the word of God like according to Psalm 119:105? According to Romans 1:16, why was Paul unashamed? How do you feel about the word of God?

   _____
   _____

6. Having learned what you have about the Scriptures, are you willing to read and study them? Why or why not?

   _____
   _____

Chapter Two – Words

7. What did you learn in this lesson, and how will you apply it to your life?

_____
_____

SCRIPTURE

Psalm 1:1-3　　　　　　　　　Psalm 119　　　　　　　　　Romans 1:16

Proverbs 4:20-22　　　　　　Hebrews 4:12　　　　　　　2 Timothy 3:16

2 Peter 1:20-21　　　　　　　Exodus 20:1-17　　　　　　Exodus 32:15-16

CHAPTER THREE

GOD

Chapter Three – God

So far, we've discovered two important truths: God can be known, and God has revealed himself. So here's the next question: Who *is* this God?

See, it doesn't work to simply say "I believe in God." If we're going to build a bridge from doctrine to life, then we'd better know what kind of God we're talking about.

Previously, we made a distinction between the two ways God reveals himself to us – through general revelation (a basic revelation about God known to all, like his existence, power, etc., which can be observed through nature)[45] and through special revelation (a more complete revelation of God to us through Scripture and miracles)[46]. Having now thought through some good reasons to trust the Scriptures, let's learn how they describe God.

THE PERSONAL ABSOLUTE

God is not a force. He is personal, sort of like you. But, God is not a person like you. God has absolute, total power and authority. And those two ideas – the personhood of God and the absolute power and authority of God – are difficult to remember.

When we forget, even for a moment, that God is fundamentally personal, we approach knowing him the same way we approach knowing our computers: push the correct keys of religious observance, contrition, etc., and you'll get the outputs of blessing, happiness, or whatever else you want.

When we forget, even for a moment, that God is absolute, we make a different set of mistakes.[47] Some may think of God as their buddy – a big brother who can beat up the bully down the street. He's not omnipotent, omniscient, or holy. But, he's super cool with me and my problems, man. So, we end up with a god who is personal, but frankly useless. He's powerless to help, win, or be victorious over the problems which plague us and our world. He's so like us that all of sudden he no longer resembles God.

So it always goes with the gods men invent. One man will invent for himself a god who is infinitely powerful, supremely strong, and completely other than himself, only to find out that the god he's invented is so different from him that he can't really say he knows anything about him. This god is so "other" than us that he could never get his hands dirty with us and our issues. Seeing this problem, another man will seek to soothe us by telling us of a god who is near to us, and can deeply identify with our pain, problems, and questions. This god turns out to be so common, however, that he can't be said to have anything to do or say about the problems of the human condition, evil, or suffering. Since this kind of god is so similar to us, it's pointless of us to ask much of him.

---

[45] Packer, J. I. *Concise Theology : A Guide to Historic Christian Beliefs.* Wheaton, Ill.: Tyndale House, 1995.

[46] Dockery, David S., Trent C. Butler, Christopher L. Church et al. *Holman Bible Handbook*, p 6. Nashville, TN: Holman Bible Publishers, 1992.

[47] I am speaking here of those who have committed themselves to doing anything they can or must do to make God more and more present in the world. Such an overemphasis on the immanence of God can be found in open theism, or forms of panentheism like process theology, etc. These are attempts to have God be in solidarity with the human condition while not in any (or very many, at least) way(s) absolute over it.

God – Chapter Three

But, the God of the Bible is both absolute (totally powerful, supreme, wise, and holy) and personal (knowable and relatable). Every other world religion emphasizes one of these qualities over the other, but only in the Scriptures do we find a God who is the great Personal Absolute. And he turns out to be better than we could possibly imagine.

> **What does "Personal Absolute" mean, and how does that phrase help us avoid errors in thinking about God?**
>
> *He is knowable & relatable & also totally powerful, supreme, wise, & holy.*

GOD IS GREAT

In the movie *Rudy*, the wise Father Cavanaugh, trying to encourage our downtrodden hero, says to Rudy, "Son, in 35 years of religious study, I have only come up with two hard incontrovertible facts: there is a God, and I'm not him." He's exactly right.

> *Hear, O Israel: The LORD our God, the LORD is one. To you it was shown, that you might know that the LORD is God; there is no other besides him. But I am the LORD your God from the land of Egypt; you know no God but me, and besides me there is no savior.*
> (Deuteronomy 6:4, 4:35, Hosea 13:4).

In John 17:3, Jesus himself adds, "And this is eternal life, that they only know you the only true God ..."

God is well-committed to the idea that he is the *only* true God. In fact, Scripture is replete with the declarations that any other claims to divinity are false. Something or someone who claims to be like God is an idol, and that claim is a lie.

> *They have made me jealous with what is no god; they have provoked me to anger with their idols.*
> (Deuteronomy 32:21).

> *For all the gods of the peoples are worthless idols, but the LORD made the heavens.* (Psalm 96:5).

> *Who is like you, majestic in holiness, awesome in glorious deeds, doing wonders?* (Exodus 15:11).

> *Therefore you are great, O LORD God. For there is none like you, and there is no God besides you, according to all that we have heard with our ears,*
> (2 Samuel 7:22).

Chapter Three – God

The greatnesses of God are the superlatives (all-powerful, all-knowing, all-sovereign, etc.) which are precisely those parts of his nature that are most unlike us. He is, simply put, greater than we are in every way.

As the Personal Absolute, God is completely self-sufficient. Unlike us, he does not depend on anything for his existence. He exists totally and utterly independently, all on his own. You need food, water, and shelter. God doesn't. We are utterly dependent from birth on our parents, our environment, and a million other things. I mean, some of us can't even make it through the day without our barista making us an overpriced coffee. For goodness sakes, we are *not* independent.

> *The God who made the world and everything in it, being Lord of Heaven and Earth, does not live in temples made by man, nor is He served by human hands, as though he needed anything, since He himself gives to all mankind life and breath and everything.*
> (Acts 17:24-25).

What wonderful news! God wants to be in relationship with us. He doesn't need us, he wants us! He doesn't desire our worship because he's lonely or has self-esteem issues, but because relationship with him is worshipful life. He is the source from which we draw life, breath, and everything. Just as the source of a ray's warmth and light is in the sun, so the source of our life and joy should be in God. And yet, this self-existent God wants to relate to us. He radiates upon us not like an impersonal sun, but like the face of a loving father gazing at his children.

The story of Moses gives us an amazing insight into God's self-existence. Recalling the scene, we find Moses, a scared shepherd who recently fled prosecution and a broken past in Egypt to the deserts of Midian. His job occupied the bottom of the social ladder: sheep boy. That's a pretty steep drop from prince of Egypt. In the middle of his mundane job, God appears to him with the strangest and most sublime introduction.

"Who are you?" he asks God. "What should I call you?"

God's reply? "I AM that I AM." (Exodus 3:14)

At the most foundational level, God is the One who is. There has never been a time that God has not been there. It's not just that he was, or even that he will always be. He is. Eternally, infinitely, and most basically, he *is*. Why is this good news? Michael Horton explains:

> *It is precisely in God's independence and freedom from contingency that a habitable space is opened for the freedom of contingent reality. If the world is not God's body, it is nevertheless God's house. Yet it is a place for us to have fellowship with him rather than a temple that he needs or that can contain him (Acts 17: 24-26).*[48]

Summarizing, here are some of the attributes of God we've explored:

- Omnipotence – God is all-powerful.
- Independence – God is self-sufficient and doesn't depend on anyone or anything for life.

---

[48] Horton, Michael S. (2011-01-04). The Christian Faith: A Systematic Theology for Pilgrims on the Way (Kindle Locations 5630-5632). Zondervan. Kindle Edition.

Read Matthew 19:26. Does this verse give you confidence in God? Why?

Yes b/c nothing is impossible for Him. However, I still need to battle with things I want vs things God wants. (this disconnect clearly stems from my lack of faith & knowledge though...)

LIMITLESS, POWERFUL, WISE, AND TRUE

We're limited by all kinds of factors: gravity, physics, our bodies, and time. But if God created all things, then he necessarily cannot be limited by them. Such independent power naturally makes us think about his infinite, mind-blowing wisdom, intelligence, and a hundred other aspects of his nature. That's how it is with God – all his attributes connect. He stands outside and separate from the physical universe, because he made it.

And what is in this universe? In a word, everything. Everything physical, anyway. Every star, of which there are over 300 sextillion[49] (that's 3×10^{23}), every galaxy, of which there are over 125 billion,[50] even down to every molecule (which there are estimated to be 10^{82} – that's 10 with 82 more zeros after it). All of this, the Scriptures tell us, is sustained by God (Heb. 1:3). Can you imagine the sheer power required to bring about such an unsearchable amount of matter and space? Can even our best minds conceive of such vastness? I certainly cannot wrap my mind around a number with 82 zeroes after it. How much less, then, can I comprehend the strength of the God of who brought it all about. God's power is unimaginably great and earns God the description *all-powerful*.

Since God is not limited by the universe He created, He isn't just powerful, but also without any physical limitation. There's nowhere he cannot be, yet nowhere can fully contain Him. He is limitless – or put another way, He is eternal. The Bible describes this God living "from everlasting to everlasting," (Ps. 90:2) – being without any kind of beginning or end.

Every kid asks their parents (at least, I know mine have), "Daddy, where did God come from? Does God have a mommy and daddy?" I love this question, but even though the answer is simple, it's profound: God has no beginning or end. There was never a time when God was not. Our lives involve the succession of one moment to the next. This is the scaffolding upon which God has hung creation. But, he is not limited by the scaffold, or any other created structures. He is eternal in existence and has no limit to his being.

All of these absolute attributes (absolute power, absolute existence, etc.) relate to and touch each other. For instance, because God is eternal, there's not a moment in which he's not present, nor will there be a moment of our lives in which God isn't

---

[49] Dennis Bodzash, "300 Sextillion Stars," *The Examiner*, December 2, 2010, http://www.examiner.com/article/300-sextillion-stars-major-nasa-announcement-about-alien-life-today (accessed September 13, 2012).

[50] "Nasa Answers: How Many Galaxies Are There?" Nasa, http://imagine.gsfc.nasa.gov/docs/ask_astro/answers/021127a.html (accessed September 13, 2012).

Chapter Three – God

already there waiting for us. Because God is powerful, there's nothing we can ask that's outside of his ability to do. Therefore, it stands to reason that there's not one bit of reality that God doesn't know, not one truth that God doesn't understand, and not one future event in which God is not already present, waiting to be known.

> *I am God, and there is no other; I am God, and there is none like me, declaring the end from the beginning and from ancient times things not yet done, saying, "My counsel shall stand, and I will accomplish my purpose."* (Isaiah 46:9-10).

In this passage, God pins his divinity on his absolute power over creation. He sees it. He knows it. He tells it what to do, and it obeys his will.

And that fact brings us to another aspect of God's power – his sovereignty. *Sovereign* is a kingly, majestic word. When we describe God as "sovereign," what we're saying is that God is king, and he rules over all things, all people, all times, all places, all preferences, and all actions. Considering the sovereignty of God has the dual effect of bringing us great comfort, because there's nothing over which God does not rule, and yet also some concern. When we start considering how free and strong God is, we begin to see ourselves rightly. We're not that strong, and we're not that sovereign. A.W. Pink puts it this way:

> *What do we mean by [the sovereignty of God]? We mean the supremacy of God, the kingship of God, the god-hood of God. To say that God is Sovereign is to declare that God is God. To say that God is Sovereign is to declare that He is the Most High, doing according to His will in the army of Heaven, and among the inhabitants of the earth, so that none can stay His hand or say unto Him what doest Thou? (Dan. 4:35). To say that God is Sovereign is to declare that He is the Almighty, the Possessor of all power in Heaven and earth, so that none can defeat His counsels, thwart His purpose, or resist His will (Psa. 115:3). To say that God is Sovereign is to declare that He is "The Governor among the nations" (Psa. 22:28), setting up kingdoms, overthrowing empires, and determining the course of dynasties as pleaseth Him best. To say that God is Sovereign is to declare that He is the "Only Potentate, the King of kings, and Lord of lords" (1 Tim. 6:15). Such is the God of the Bible.*[51]

So, here's a summary of the amazing attributes of God we've just explored:

- Omniscience – God knows all truth, and everything that will happen.
- Eternality – God isn't limited by time, space, or matter. He is eternal and infinite.
- Sovereignty – God alone rules and reigns, and his will is always accomplished.

> **Re-read the Scriptures in this section. How do they make you feel? What questions do they bring up?**
>
> *I realize literally everything SCREAMS the existence of God. And yet, here I am, feeling human emotions & doubts.*

---

[51] A. W. Pink, *The Sovereignty of God*, chapter 1.

SPIRITUAL, HOLY, AND GOOD

*[Handwritten note: what is culture, & how does the monolithic nature of God separate from that?
1. we must assume that the existence of God is true.]*

Thinking about God's power, might, knowledge, and wisdom is awesome. Having been created in his image, though, there are also many attributes of God that we can more easily relate to. Sometimes these are called God's knowable, shared, or communicable attributes.

The personal nature of the absolute God is a subject of considerable wonder, especially given all the ways we, in some limited way, resemble the limitless beauty of God. One such attribute is the spirituality of God. Now, I don't mean here that God is religious or meditates; that's how we use the word. I'm talking here about the fact that God is spirit. [52]

He is present in the world but not in a way that is weighable, touchable, or able to be experimented upon. He is Spirit. "Now wait," you may say. "If we can't see him how do we know he is there?" Good question. Reflect on that for a moment, and I think you'll find that there are all kinds of things you know exist that are not material things. Your mind, for instance, is a nonmaterial thing. I'm not talking about your brain, I'm talking about that which is essentially your thought. Thought is a nonphysical phenomenon – or at least not a purely physical one. Not convinced? How about numbers. We all agree numbers exist. But, please show me how much 326 weighs. What does it smell like? What happens when you dip it in water? Nothing, of course, because it's nonphysical. See, you always knew non-material things existed. Similarly, God is a nonphysical being.

The fact that God is spirit is good news. It means that our desire to live forever can be realized. We have been made in the image of our personal Creator – spiritual. And, spiritual connection with God involves all kinds of other connections – moral, relational, and devotional.

For instance, whenever we observe anything and label it "good," we're making reference to God, who is absolute goodness. There isn't some standard of goodness out there somewhere that God is just really good at conforming to. Nor does God get to arbitrarily decide what will be called "good" today – a decision that might change tomorrow. Because God is the Personal Absolute, we come to understand that *he* is the standard. This also means that everything God does is worthy of praise and approval. Of course, that's a message that we don't like to hear these days. What we are willing to call good is much more closely attached to our preferences, our culture, and our time. But with God, this is simply not the case. Goodness, truth, beauty – these ideas are all fixed in God himself. While we may change, God does not. Therefore, what is actually good, right, true, and beautiful will never change.

But God's goodness begs us to ask a question: How good, exactly, is God? The answer: completely. He is complete, total, and essential goodness. That means that God is totally separate from the stains of impatience, brokenness, and dysfunction – and this kind of unique goodness has a name: holiness.

The holiness of God means that he is unstained by evil and always devoted to the highest good. Holiness means that God is both separate from something (sin and depravity) and oriented toward something (complete goodness.) We can easily imagine that God is separate from evil, but have we also considered that he is utterly devoted to the greatest cosmic good? In fact, he is. God is passionately, infinitely, and completely committed to the highest good imaginable.

And, what (or rather, who) is the highest good imaginable? God.

---

[52] John 4:24, "God is spirit, and those who worship him must worship in spirit and in truth."

Chapter Three – God

Initially, that may sound mind-bending. If I walked up to you and introduced myself by saying, "Hello, my name is Adam, and I'm committed to the highest good in the universe ... me," then you'd accuse me of being a self-centered jerk. What kind of person calls themselves the greatest, best, and most perfect thing the cosmos has ever seen? Well, God does. In fact, only God can say that, because only God is, in fact, the best being imaginable. You see, if were committed to myself as the highest good, I'm committed to something that's just not true. I'm *not* actually the greatest being imaginable. Oh sure, I'm unique, special, and all that other stuff my first grade teacher said I was. But, we're all pretty certain that we're not the greatest beings in the universe.

The awareness of that fact should tell us something. At some depth within ourselves to which we may not have yet even descended, we know that Someone is actually great, good, and glorious. It's just not us.

Knowledge of this kind explains why we're not impressed when impostors try to convince us of their greatness. We may go along with them for a bit, thinking that they are truly great. Perhaps it's a celebrity we follow, only to find that behind the stage lights her life is a wreck. Maybe it's a politician who promises change, only we find that he's not the messiah he promised he'd be. It could even be a man or woman we're dating, but we're finding out that they're not all they're cracked up to be. These impostors aren't meant to teach us that there's no such thing as a truly good person, just that there's only one truly good Person – the Absolute Person. His true, complete, and utter goodness means that he's different from us. He's holy.

Holiness means that God is free from the grime of sin and sadness, but it also means more. God is totally special and different. And as such, God is devoted at the deepest level to his glory – that is, the manifestation of all these different magnificences: independence, goodness, power, etc. What's more, he wants us to experience his glory as something different from and better than anything else. That is part of what David means when he tells us to "taste and see that the LORD is good," (Ps. 34:8).

God doesn't merely require that we shut up, submit, and serve Him. God's goodness means that our highest good is to be found in relationship to Him. Knowing him is great, because no one is greater than him. Reviewing, here are the attributes we've mentioned:

- Spiritual – God is Spirit.
- Goodness – God is always good, and goodness is found in God.
- Holiness – God is set apart from the world and sin that stains it.

What is an attribute about God you learned in this section for the first time? How does it affect you?

_____

_____

_____

JUST AND RIGHT

Everyone everywhere has within them some sort of moral compass. If you think hard enough right now, you can probably come up with something that's going on somewhere on the planet that you'd describe as wrong – something that should be stopped. Where does such a sense of justice come from? Well, from God. God is just and right in all he does. Therefore, the beings he creates bear a sense of justice.

> *The LORD, the LORD, a God merciful and gracious, slow to anger, and abounding in steadfast love and faithfulness, keeping love for thousands, forgiving iniquity and transgression and sin, but who will by no means clear the guilty, visiting the iniquity of the fathers on the children and the children's children, to the third and the fourth generation. (Exodus 34:6b-7)*

It's hard for some to believe that God is both good and just. But, we must remember that all of the attributes we've been discussing are connected. Theologian Michael Horton says it this way:

> *God always exercises his power, holiness, righteousness, and wrath – as well as his love and mercy – in conformity with his goodness. In fact, we could hardly affirm God's goodness if he did not uphold justice and the cause of his righteousness against sin and evil.*[53]

Some protest by saying that if we teach that God is just, righteous, and takes out all the bad guys, then we might just as well go and take out some bad guys ourselves. Doesn't belief in a God of justice have a propensity to make us violent? I don't believe so. I would argue that without belief in the God revealed in the Scriptures – the loving, totally just, merciful, and mighty God that Jesus Christ talked about and gave his life to reveal – we have no recourse but to be the enforcers of justice ourselves. Consider what Miroslav Volf says about such an idea:

> *If God were not angry at injustice and deception and did not make a final end to violence – that God would not be worthy of worship ... The only means of prohibiting all recourse to violence by ourselves is to insist that violence is legitimate only when it comes from God ... My thesis that the practice of nonviolence requires a belief in divine vengeance will be unpopular with many ... in the West ... [But] it takes the quiet of a suburban home for the birth of the thesis that human nonviolence [results from the belief in] God's refusal to judge. In a sun-scorched land, soaked in the blood of the innocent, it will invariably die ... [with] other pleasant captivities of the liberal mind.*[54]

Because God is just, we can trust him to settle injustice in the world. In a world beset with racism, classism, war, poverty, and disease, it is comforting to know that God will deal rightly with all people, not allowing the guilty to go unpunished, but providing love and mercy to those who turn from unrighteousness and to him for forgiveness.

To review then, we discovered that God is:

---

[53] Horton, Michael S. (2011-01-04). *The Christian Faith: A Systematic Theology for Pilgrims on the Way* (Kindle Locations 6516-6518). Zondervan. Kindle Edition.

[54] Miroslav Volf, *Exclusion and Embrace: A Theological Exploration of Identity, Otherness, and Reconciliation*, Abingdon, 1996, 303-304. Quoted from Tim Keller, *The Reason for God*, NY, NY: Dutton, 2008, 74.

Chapter Three – God

- Just and Righteous – He is always right, always does what is right, and will bring about justice.

> **Read Exodus 35:6-7. What is God's commitment to justice like?**
> _____
> _____
> _____

ALWAYS FULLY HIMSELF

In a culture where stories of lying, cheating, divorce, and deception are so familiar, it's difficult to conceive of a God who never, ever changes. According to the Scriptures, he is the same yesterday, today, and forever (Heb. 13:8). His promises will always stand because he never goes back on his word (Is. 40:8). This is in no way like us. We change all the time. We forget, drop the ball, lie, cheat, and change our minds. God doesn't. He is the one who declares the end from the beginning (Is. 46:10). He sets his plan, he executes his will, and he lives completely consistent with his nature.

Since we're talking about the nature of God, it can be easy to think of God like a pie: the big slice is his love, of course (mainly because we like that idea), and smaller slices of the pie are his lesser appreciated attributes (holiness, power, etc.). But of course, God isn't a pie and his attributes aren't slices. God is fully himself. He is fully powerful, fully loving, fully wise. God is fully himself in all of his ways, which is wonderful news for us.

Isn't it excellent to know that God will never get up on the wrong side of the bed? Every good, beautiful, and excellent thing in life comes from God, who never, ever changes (James 1:17). This means that God is:

- Unchangeable – While God acts in history, his person, promises, and perfections never change.

> **Why is it good news that God never changes? How does this impact your relationship to him?**
> _____
> _____
> _____

THE UNITY AND COMMUNITY OF LOVE

One final attribute remains. More than all the others, this attribute is the one that almost everyone agrees upon and almost everyone misunderstands. I'm talking of course about the love of God. Consider what New Testament scholar D.A. Carson, says on the topic:

> *If people believe in God at all today, the overwhelming majority hold that this God – however he, she, or it may be understood – is a loving being ... [T]his widely disseminated belief in the love of God is set with increasing frequency in some matrix other than [a biblical one]. The result is that when informed Christians talk about the love of God, they mean something very different from what is meant in the surrounding culture. Worse, neither side may perceive that that is the case.*[55]

What does it mean to say that God is love? Not merely that he is lov*ing*, but that he *is* love. Consider how fervently the Apostle John makes the case:

> *Anyone who does not love does not know God, because God is love. In this the love of God was made manifest among us, that God sent his only Son into the world, so that we might live through him. In this is love, not that we have loved God but that he loved us and sent his Son to be the propitiation for our sins. Beloved, if God so loved us, we also ought to love one another. No one has ever seen God; if we love one another, God abides in us and his love is perfected in us. By this we know that we abide in him and he in us, because he has given us of his Spirit. And we have seen and testify that the Father has sent his Son to be the Savior of the world. Whoever confesses that Jesus is the Son of God, God abides in him, and he in God. So we have come to know and to believe the love that God has for us. God is love, and whoever abides in love abides in God, and God abides in him.* (1 John 4:8-16)

In John's mind, the case is quite clear. God is love, and without knowing God we misunderstand what love is in the first place. We need to ask, what is the love of God? Does it mean that he's got nice feelings toward us? Or, is it perhaps that God's love is conditional? We do good, and he loves us ... until we stop doing good, of course.

The single greatest demonstration of the love of God was mentioned by the Apostle John in the previous passage. If we were to ask John how God has shown his love for humanity, then John would answer, "By sending his son Jesus into the world to die for our sins." For John, a man who walked with Jesus, witnessed his agony on the cross, and then his resurrection, there was no greater way God has demonstrated his love for us than the life, death, and resurrection of Jesus.

This should tell us something about the love of God. Namely, that it is extraordinarily costly to God while being totally free to us. God's love isn't needy. It's not some kind of codependency where we love God and then he loves us back. No, God's love is the kind which seeks out those who are far away from him, even though it costs him the life of the Son. This is what God has done, in history, to show us his love. That means that the love of God is something far more than mere sentimentality. It's precious, powerful, transformational, costly, and totally free for us.

- Love – God is love, overflowing with self-giving affection.

---

[55] D.A. Carson, *The Difficult Doctrine of the Love of God*. Great Britain: Intervarsity, 2000, 10.

Chapter Three – God

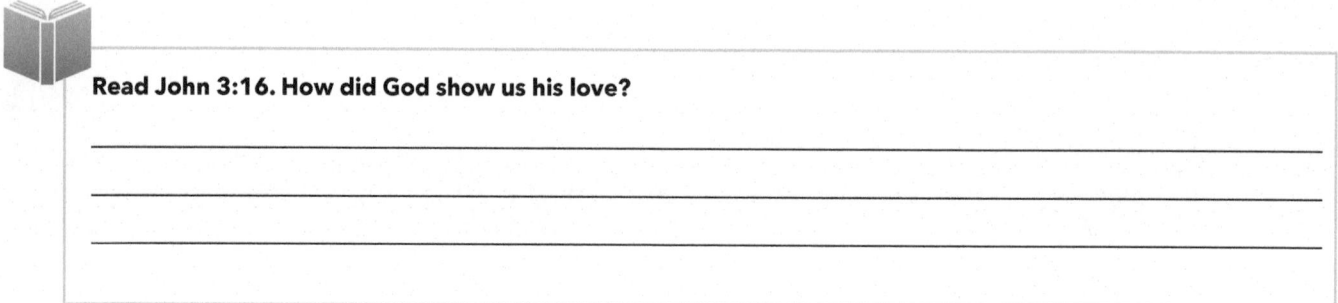

Read John 3:16. How did God show us his love?

_____
_____
_____

TRINITY

Until now, we've described God as both personal and absolute. These have been our two watchwords while we've considered his nature. But, the Scriptures reveal something further about God, something entirely necessary and utterly amazing that we call the Trinity.

Trinity means that there is one God who eternally exists in three persons, or centers of personality.

That means that God is both unity and community, both one and three. In his essence, God is one. But, in his personhood, God is three: Father, Son, and Holy Spirit. One God, three persons. But how can this be? How can God be both one *and* three? What does oneness even mean for God? In his book *Delighting in the Trinity,* Michael Reeves writes:

> *Oneness for the single-person God would mean sameness. Alone for eternity without any beside him, why would he value others and their differences? ... Oneness for the triune God means unity. As the Father is absolutely one with his Son, and yet is not his Son, so Jesus prays that believers might be one, but not that they might all be the same.*[56]

Oneness doesn't mean sameness, it means unity.

For nearly the first four hundred years following the death and resurrection of Jesus, the topic of the Trinity was *the* hot-button issue of theological debate. How God's people were to understand the nature of God as one God in three persons was to occupy nearly all the theological energy of the church fathers. Settling this issue was not only a major accomplishment for our understanding of God, but for the story of the Gospel itself.

---

[56] Reeves, Michael (2012-07-03). *Delighting in the Trinity: An Introduction to the Christian Faith* (p. 103). InterVarsity Press. Kindle Edition.

But, before you begin to think that some early church fathers made this up, let's take a look at the Scriptures. As we do, we notice that the Scriptures ascribe divinity not only to God the Father, but also to the Son and the Holy Spirit. Of the Father, the Scriptures say:

> *Do not labor for the food that perishes, but for the food that endures to eternal life, which the Son of Man will give to you. For on him God the Father has set his seal.* (John 6:27)

> *[Y]et for us there is one God, the Father, from whom are all things and for whom we exist.* (1 Corinthians 8:6)

> And another says, *Blessed be the God and Father of our Lord Jesus Christ …* (Ephesians 1:3).

Continue reading, however, and you'll quickly bump into Scriptures where the Holy Spirit is referred to as God as well. He is not some impersonal force-like gravity. He is a person of the Godhead. He is called eternal in the book of Hebrews (Heb. 9:14). David speaks of his omnipresence when he writes, "Where shall I go from your Spirit? Or where shall I flee from your presence?" (Ps. 139:7) Isaiah writes of his infinite knowledge in the creation of the world, saying, "Who has measured the Spirit of the LORD, or what man shows him his counsel? Whom did he consult, and who made him understand?" (Is. 40:13-14a) This all-powerful, personal, present-at-creation, omniscient Person sure does sound a lot like God.

But by far the most controversial idea within Christianity is the claim that the Scriptures make about Jesus – that he is fully divine, the Son of God. This inescapable truth is affirmed all across the Scriptures, and provides the final clarifying piece to the Trinitarian puzzle. It's clear that Jesus was, according to all the biblical writers, considered divine in his nature (one God), but yet somehow distinct from his Father (three persons). This is such a critical piece that Reeves notes that since God is, before all things, a Father, and not primarily Creator or Ruler, all his ways are beautifully fatherly.[57]

The Bible tells us that Jesus was worshipped by God-fearing Jews as their Lord and God, "And behold, Jesus met them and said, 'Greetings!' And they came up and took hold of his feet and worshiped him," (Matt. 28:9). John's gospel describes Jesus as the eternal Word through which everything and everyone was made.

> *In the beginning was the Word, and the Word was with God, and the Word was God. He was in the beginning with God. All things were made through him, and without him was not any thing made that was made. In him was life, and the life was the light of men.* (John 1:1-4).

Some have tried to argue that Jesus never thought of himself as God's Son. But, that doesn't seem to be the case either, since he often called God his Father (something that Jews never did), and was eventually killed for it.

> *But Jesus answered them, "My Father is working until now, and I am working." This was why the Jews were seeking all the more to kill him, because not only was he breaking the Sabbath, but he was even calling God his own Father, making himself equal with God. So Jesus said to them, "Truly, truly, I say to you, the Son can do nothing of his own accord, but only what he sees the Father doing. For whatever the Father does, that the Son does likewise. For the Father loves the Son and shows him all that he himself is doing. And greater works than these will he show him, so that you may marvel. For as the Father raises the dead and gives them life, so also the Son gives life to whom he will. The Father judges no one, but has given all*

---

[57] Reeves, Michael (2012-07-03). *Delighting in the Trinity: An Introduction to the Christian Faith* (p. 103). InterVarsity Press. Kindle Edition.

Chapter Three – God

judgment to the Son, that all may honor the Son, just as they honor the Father. Whoever does not honor the Son does not honor the Father who sent him. (John 5:17-23).

The Scriptures bring us to the inescapable and amazing conclusion that God is one and God is three ... and that is wonderful news.

> **Read Matthew 28:18-20. What do the words of Jesus teach you about the nature of God as Trinity?**
> _____
> _____
> _____

WHY DOES TRINITY MATTER?

I remember leading a discussion on a university about the doctrine of the Trinity. After a brief (and what I thought was a pretty good) explanation of much of what you just read, one young man said, "I get it. I believe it, but if I'm honest, I'm just not sure at all why this matters." Many well meaning Christians probably land here. The Trinity is an idea we agree with, but not a doctrine that really impacts life. But if we look closer, we'll see that without this precious doctrine life with God looks very different, and very bad for us.

First, if God is not Trinity, then he created us out of loneliness and need. Think of this for a moment: If God is simply one person all alone, then how can he love? How can he be good? How can he be kind and gracious? Answer: he cannot, because those attributes can only exist in community. Love requires another, because love does not exist without demonstration. If God is not Trinity, then God is not loving. Sure, he may become loving. He may develop kindness. But these attributes cannot be essential to his nature unless they are eternally expressed.

But we know that God is eternally happy in the love and community of the Trinity. God is very pleased with his Son. The Son is passionate about the Father. All the persons of the Trinity unite in a self-giving unity and community of love and life. If God were not this way then God would not be able to be loving until he had something or someone to love.

Second, if God is not Trinity then we don't know how to live together. Because God is both unity and community, we have a good reason to organize life accordingly. In a world of political and social brokenness, we can easily see what happens when individuals are sacrificed for the good of the community or state. We only need look as far back as World War II to find out what happens when a society decides that a certain group of individuals is undesirable. The killing fields of Cambodia, the concentration camps of Dachau and Auschwitz – these stand as monuments to the idea of the supremacy of the society at the expense of the individual. If God is simply one without internal diversity, then we would have no way to justify the rights of individuals in communities.

However, today we live in an age when the rights of individuals are so over-preferred that a single person's preferences, feelings, and proclivities can change the course of the entire society, because the individual is the basic unit of society, or so it is said. If there were three separate gods, then we would have no theology to support a strong community. But, because within God there is unity *and* diversity, and we are made in his image, we have a means to hold in balance the rights of individuals *and* needs of communities. God's very nature gives us a great resource to develop a proper understanding of the balance of a civilization and its parts. Without this, what anchor have we against tyranny of the state or the citizen?

Finally, and most importantly, if Jesus Christ isn't fully God and fully man then he cannot save anyone from anything. This is perhaps the most important practical application of the Trinity. If Jesus Christ is a created being and not God, then it is hard (if not impossible) to see how he, a created being, could bear the full wrath of God against all our sins, or live the completely perfect, untouched-by-sin kind of life that is demanded by the perfection of God. Suffice it to say for now that, according to the Scriptures, the infinite nature of humanity's debt is such that it must be paid with an infinitely worthy payment. Only one person is of infinite worth: God himself. So, if Jesus Christ is not God, and not eternally good and righteous, then it would be impossible for him to pay an eternal debt, namely that of the brokenness of humanity.

What is one practical application of understanding God as Trinity that sticks with you from this section?

_____

_____

_____

THE GOD OF THE STORY

The limitless goodness, holiness, and beauty of God means that if we come to know this Divine Being – Father, Son, and Holy Spirit – then we will find ourselves in relationship with One who is unable to be exhausted for all his wonder. We'll never get bored of looking at him because there's always more of him to see. We'll never tire of hearing him speak because there will always be more of him to know. These precious doctrines about God cannot help but shape life.

And yet, the world which we currently occupy seems to be somewhat absent of all this wonder, doesn't it? On some level we find beauty in creation. We love nature, people, romance, music, and all the other good things about creation. Yet in our wonder, we also find in these things the potential for harm and pain. How did this story – our story – come about? What is the relationship of God, this Personal Absolute, to me, you, and the rest of the universe?

Why did God make us? How can we know him? Why does it seem like so many of us don't have a clue about him? These questions drive us to the next part of our journey as the story of God's great love for his people gets underway – a story which begins with the gracious gift of creation.

Chapter Three – God

APPLICATION & REFLECTION

1. Of the attributes of God mentioned in this chapter, which is easiest to understand? Which seems more difficult to understand? Why?

   _____
   _____
   _____

2. According to Isaiah 46:9-10, how many gods are there? How does God express his power here? Why is this verse good news?

   _____
   _____
   _____

3. What does Trinity mean? Why does it matter?

   _____
   _____
   _____

4. Of the three reasons the Trinity is an important truth listed above, which one speaks to you most? Why?

   the community + individuality aspect
   _____
   _____

5. Read John 5:17-23. Describe the relationship between the Father and the Son.

   _____
   _____
   _____

6. One pastor wrote, "To know the Trinity is to know God, an eternal and personal God of infinite beauty, interest and fascination. The Trinity is a God we can know, and forever grow to know better." Respond to that statement. Do you agree? Why?

7. Read Genesis 1:26. What might it mean that humanity was made in the image of a God who is both three persons and one essence?

8. According to Deuteronomy 6:5-6 and 11:1, how is love for God expressed? What does Jesus say we will do if we love him in John 14:15? Do you love and obey God?

9. What in this chapter most surprised you to learn about God? Do you feel motivated to know this God? Why?

SCRIPTURE

Exodus 3:14
Isaiah 46:9-10
Ephesians 4:4-6

Exodus 34:6-7
Acts 2:33
Deuteronomy 6:5-6, 11:1

1 John 4:16
1 Corinthians 8:6
John 14:15

Chapter Three – God

SECTION TWO

GRACE

CHAPTER FOUR

ORIGIN

Chapter Four – Origin

History is the manuscript upon which God has written. So we learn about God as we explore the story of story that sweeps all the way through the Scriptures. And like all stories, this one has a beginning.

ORIGINS AND ORIENTATION

In the greatest stories, the first few lines set the reader up for the rest of his journey. Our story is the same. What we understand about our origins sets up and informs our orientation – where we think we're going. And our story – the story of everything and everyone – starts with God.

> *In the beginning, God ... (Genesis 1:1)*

God appears as the main character. But, he doesn't merely appear. He does something. The very next word tells us God's relationship to everything else in the world. It's the word, "creates." God creates. Those two words, "God creates," are foundations that many wish to reject. But, the distinction is clear – a distinction between the Creator and creature.

The way we view our origins colors the glasses through which we understand our orientation. We call these "glasses" worldviews. Largely speaking, these world-views fall into two categories – though there are many nuanced versions of each. One is called naturalism and the other is called pantheism.

Why does our view of the beginning of the story matter so much?
_____
_____
_____

THE FALSE VIEW OF NATURALISM

One of the chief competitors to the Christian worldview, naturalism states that all reality is contained in nature and is able to be exhaustively understood by the scientific method.[58] The naturalist credo is roughly the same as the kangaroo in Dr. Suess' *Horton Hears a Who*, "If I can't touch it or see it, it doesn't exist!"

---

[58] David Papineau, "Naturalism", *The Stanford Encyclopedia of Philosophy (Spring 2009 Edition)*, Edward N. Zalta (ed.), URL = <http://plato.stanford.edu/archives/spr2009/entries/naturalism/>.

I remember being a boy and watching *Cosmos*, hosted by famous atheistic naturalist Carl Sagan. His summary of the worldview of naturalism was succinct and sounded almost biblical: "The universe is all that is, was, or ever will be." On this view, anything that isn't testable through the scientific method (that is, anything nonphysical, spiritual) simply doesn't exist. No need to *prove* it doesn't exist; according to naturalism it can't possibly exist. With this way of looking at our origins, God is kicked out before we even get started because nothing like God can possibly be there. Naturalism is a system of *one-ism*. In this worldview there's only one kind of thing – nature. You might picture naturalism as a circle. Inside the circle you'll find all physical reality; weighable, touchable, seeable, measurable, scientifically-inquireable matter. Anything that can't go into the box labeled "nature" isn't allowed to exist.

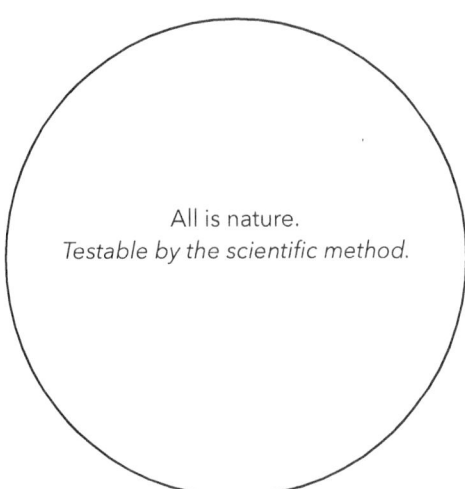

All is nature.
Testable by the scientific method.

So what does this worldview say about the beginning of everything? How does it account for the start of the story? One famous naturalist writes:

> *What does need its origin explained is the concrete Universe itself, and as Hume ... long ago asked: Why not stop at the material world? It ... does perform a version of the ultimate bootstrapping trick; it creates itself* ex nihilo. *Or at any rate out of something that is well-nigh indistinguishable from nothing at all.*[59]

The universe just happened, apparently.

Naturalism says that the world and matter came into existence through natural processes, out of nothing, for no purpose. At this point you may be asking, "How?" Great question. The answer? They have no idea. Apparently, the universe performs a "bootstrapping trick" (whatever that is) and simply creates itself. Now, here you might ask another very good question like, "How can a thing create itself before it exists?" Of course, it cannot. So, our best naturalistic minds have come up with a system that makes total sense ... except for that little part about the whole universe coming into existence for no reason, by no cause, for no purpose – literally creating itself before it existed. In a recent interview, when asked how naturalistic atheists explain the origins of the universe, Richard Dawkins gave the stunning reply, "We're working on it."[60]

"We're working on it?" Really? That sure does seem like an awfully important thing to be "working on" while you preach naturalism as though it were gospel truth. As Philosopher William Lane Craig says, "Something cannot come from nothing. To claim that something can come into being from nothing is literally worse than magic."[61]

This is the starting point for naturalism – everything came into existence for no reason, by no cause, for no purpose.

Whatever explanatory power science, evolution, and rational inquiry may have as the story goes along, they don't seem to be very helpful tools for explaining the way things like science, evolution, and thought got here in the first place.

---

[59] Daniel Dennett, *Breaking the Spell*. (New York, NY: Viking, 2006), 244.

[60] Richard Dawkins on *The O'Reilly Factor*, Fox News, April 24, 2007.

[61] William Lane Craig, *How Did the Universe Begin?* <http://www.reasonablefaith.org/media/how-did-the-universe-begin-saddleback-church#ixzz4sUH5uC2w>

Chapter Four – Origin

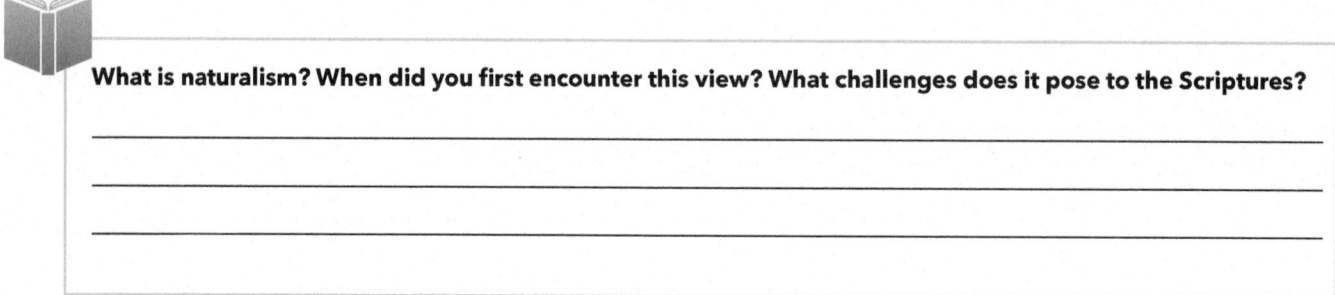

What is naturalism? When did you first encounter this view? What challenges does it pose to the Scriptures?
_____
_____
_____

THE FALSE VIEW OF PANTHEISM

The word *pantheism* from two words: *pan,* meaning "all" and *theos,* meaning "god." Like naturalism, you might picture pantheism as a circle. However, instead of the circle being labeled "nature," this one is labeled "god," or "divine." In this worldview, everything that exists is really one kind of thing, but instead of everything being non-spiritual, natural stuff, everything is super-spiritual, divine stuff. Everything from birds to tables, people to poodles, share in the same common, divine essence. All is god.

All is god.
Everything is divine.

As the view of tribal religions, Hinduism, Buddhism, and other eastern religions, pantheism is very old. Unlike the God of Scripture, there is nothing personal about divinity in pantheism. For most pantheistic religions and philosophies, the goal of life is to lose one's own personhood and self-awareness to become part of the one, impersonal, divine essence. It is to dissolve oneself into some kind of unified whole.

Initially, this sounds promising. I'm divine and so are you – how nice! But upon further consideration the whole idea begins to turn rather nasty. If everything is divine, then *everything* is divine – even bad things. It's nice to think about yourself being divine and other people being divine, but it's not so nice to think about everything being divine. Everything includes things like sickness, crime, war, murder, poverty, injustice, and a host of other terrible things. Remember the yin-yang? Part white, part black, with two dots in both parts, all meant to symbolize that in the divine essence there is both good and evil, light and darkness. All of it goes in and all of it shares in an essential divine essence.[62] As far as creation, most pantheists would say that because creation is divine, it is eternal. This, however, conflicts with modern science.[63]

---

[62] In a book like this, I can't even come close to fully treating these two worldviews, or the more nuanced worldviews that fall between them. I would encourage the reader to look into a few resources to get a fuller and more developed explanation of these systems of thought, as well as a more developed response to them. See William Lane Craig, *Reasonable Faith,* Wheaton, IL: Crossway, 2008. See also John Frame, *The Doctrine of God,* Philadelphia, PA: P&R, 1987.

[63] I'm grateful to Dr. Wayne Grudem for making these observations. For a greater expansion on the doctrine of creation from this perspective, see his extremely helpful book, *Systematic Theology,* Grand Rapids, MI: Zondervan, 1994.

What is pantheism?

_____
_____
_____

THE PROBLEMS WITH THESE VIEWS

Upon closer analysis, both of these views fall short. Naturalism takes a good shot at telling us that man came from matter already existing on the Earth, but fails totally to tell us where that matter came from. Evolution may be a compelling theory, but evolution only makes sense once you have something to evolve. It doesn't tell you where that something came from – and it never could.

Surprisingly, modern science points to a startling reality – the universe had a beginning. And, the law of causality tells us that all effects (like there being a universe, for example) need a cause – things like universes don't just happen. Words appear on this page because I typed them. The paper that makes up the book you're holding was produced from trees and other material which were processed to create it. Those trees grew in soil from seed, by a combination of light, time, genetic information, and soil. And, where did the light, time, genetic information, and soil come from? Stardust. All that we see is the exploded stuff left over from an unimaginably bright and powerful "bang" originating from an infinitesimally small point. And where, we finally ask, did that first event come from? How did it come about? Naturalism has to say, "It just happened," or "We're working on it." Naturalism leaves us either with an infinite regress of causes and effects, like dominos falling in an infinite series, or the idea that everything came from nothing with no cause, force, or purpose. Put mildly, that's crazy.

Again, William Lane Craig, a prominent philosopher, writes about this, saying:

> _On the basis of ... the finitude of the past, we have good grounds for affirming ... that the universe began to exist. From the first premise [of the argument] – that whatever begins to exist has a cause – and the second premise, [the universe began to exist], if follows logically that the universe has a cause. This conclusion ought to stagger us, to fill us with awe, for it means that the universe was brought into existence by something which is greater than and beyond it._[64]

The naturalist must believe that everything – literally _everything_ – arose from nothing, by no cause, for no purpose. People came from nothing. Consciousness came from nothing. Numbers came from nothing. Logic came from nothing. Mind came from nothing. Curious, since naturalism is usually the worldview championed by more scientifically minded people. Presumably, scientists tend to like repeatable, observable data from which to draw their conclusions. Yet, the only conclusion that we can draw from all the data of our own experience is that the only thing that comes from nothing is, well, nothing.

---

[64] Craig, _Reasonable Faith_, 150.

Chapter Four – Origin

Worse than not being able to explain the beginning, naturalism is useless to explain where the story ought to be going. If the universe and everything in it is purposeless, meaningless, valueless, and eventually headed toward an entropic heat death,[65] then nothing matters. Atheism leads to meaninglessness because the beginning of the narrative of naturalism starts with accident, not intent. There's no purpose to the universe, so nothing that happens within it (like what happens to you, for example) matters. That's not to say that all atheists actually believe the universe is meaningless. Most people have a sense of meaning that is inescapable, atheists just have a terrible time trying to explain why. According to atheistic naturalism, meaning is inexplicable, temporary, and subjective.

I'm reminded of a comic I read a while back. A group of scientists approached God and said, "We don't need you anymore. We've learned to make people, plants, and animals using science."

Interested, God replied, "Oh, really? Okay. Show me." They said, "No problem. First, we just take some dirt, and then…"

"Wait." God said. They paused and looked up. God said, "Get your own dirt."

Francis Collins, co-mapper of the human genome and current director of the National Institute of Health, makes this observation about the scientific veracity of the claim that God created everything from nothing.

> *We have this very solid conclusion that the universe had an origin, the Big Bang. Fifteen billion years ago, the universe began with an unimaginably bright flash of energy from an infinitesimally small point. That implies that before that, there was nothing. I can't imagine how nature, in this case the universe, could have created itself. And the very fact that the universe had a beginning implies that someone was able to begin it. And it seems to me that had to be outside of nature.*
>
> *A second argument: When you look from the perspective of a scientist at the universe, it looks as if it knew we were coming. There are 15 constants – the gravitational constant, various constants about the strong and weak nuclear force, etc. – that have precise values. If any one of those constants was off by even one part in a million, or in some cases, by one part in a million million, the universe could not have actually come to the point where we see it. Matter would not have been able to coalesce, there would have been no galaxies, stars, planets, or people. That's a phenomenally surprising observation. It seems almost impossible that we're here. And that does make you wonder – gosh, who was setting those constants anyway? Scientists have not been able to figure that out.* [66]

Indeed, the understanding that the universe was finely tuned for precisely our kind of life is consonant with the idea of creation.[67] What we see in the Bible is God doing what naturalistic processes are unable to do: God made life, matter, and consciousness out of nothing.

---

[65] I'm referring to what most cosmologists understand will be the eventual dying out of the universe as all the stars burn up all their fuel and the universe expands to such a point that even the molecules which compose matter will be lightyears apart. In a naturalistic worldview, this is the final destiny of all things.

[66] Steve Paulson, "The Believer," *Salon* (Accessed July 14, 2010) URL= <http://www.salon.com/books/int/2006/08/07/collins/index.html>

[67] McGrath, Alister E. (2012-01-01). *Mere Apologetics: How to Help Seekers and Skeptics Find Faith* (Kindle Locations 1754-1755). Baker Publishing Group. Kindle Edition.

So, what about pantheism? What if instead of nothing being divine, everything is? Well, therein lies the first problem. If everything is divine, or a part of the ultimate, eternal reality, then everything has to be eternal. But it is a demonstrable fact that matter, time, and energy are not eternal. These are created things which, at some point, did not exist. And the problems don't stop there.

If everything is divine, then so are the really awful things. Rape? Divine. Murder? Genocide? Both divine. That simply isn't very good news to the victims of terrible injustice. But, pantheism goes a step further – it forces individuals who have suffered to understand that ultimate reality is impersonal, and so persons don't matter. On this view, matter is an illusion, and good and evil are relative. How can a worldview like this have anything helpful to say to the problems of suffering, war, starvation, and disease? In his article, "The Meaning of Suffering," Max Scheler notes,

> Unlike [pantheists], Christians believe that suffering is real, not an illusion. "There are not reinterpretations: pain is pain, it is misery; pleasure is pleasure, positive bliss, not mere 'tranquility' . . . which Buddha considered the good of goods. In Christianity there is no diminution of sensitivity, but a mellowing of the soul in totally enduring suffering."[68]

What are the problems with naturalism and pantheism that make them untenable worldviews?

WHEN GOODNESS OVERFLOWS

The Scriptures tell us that when God creates, he does so full of intentionality, brimming with meaning, and overflowing with love. Fundamentally, the Christian worldview doesn't see everything as *one* kind of thing. In Christianity, there are two circles – God, and everything God made; the creator / creature distinction we mentioned earlier.

Those two powerful words – God creates – have huge, worldview-shaping implications. If God creates, then God isn't the same as what he makes (as pantheism suggests), nor can the universe exist without God creating it (as naturalism suggests). The Scriptures tell us:

---

[68] Max Scheler, "Meaning of Suffering," p. 110. Quoted in Keller, Timothy (2013-10-01). Walking with God through Pain and Suffering (p. 28). Penguin Group US. Kindle Edition.

Chapter Four – Origin

> *In the beginning, God created the heavens and the earth. The earth was without form and void, and darkness was over the face of the deep. And the Spirit of God was hovering over the face of the waters. In the beginning was the Word, and the Word was with God, and the Word was God. He was in the beginning with God. All things were made through him, and without him was not any thing made that was made. And God saw everything that he had made, and behold, it was very good...*
> (Genesis 1:1-2, John 1:1-3, Genesis 1:31a).

Remember, God is independent, full, and happy. He doesn't need anything. So why create? Well, if it wasn't out of a lack or need, then there's only one other possible explanation – overflow. Remember, things don't just happen. Every effect that we see around us has a cause. The universe is the effect of the cause of God's will, and it is a glorious one, meant to inspire us to worship and adore God, the creator.[69]

God's creativity wasn't to fill a need or scratch an itch. He wasn't lonely, bored, or taking a risk. The creation in which we find ourselves is what happens when infinite goodness overflows with infinite power. God, in unearned kindness, made a universe capable of sustaining life like ours so that we could see it, experience it, and enjoy a loving relationship with the God who made it.

Read Psalm 33. What is this poem all about? How does it make you feel toward God's creative work?
_____
_____
_____

GOD OF THE BEGINNING

> *In the beginning, God created the heavens and the earth. The earth was without form and void, and darkness was over the face of the deep. And the Spirit of God was hovering over the face of the waters. And then God said, "Let there be light..."* (Genesis 1:1-3).

The word used for "God" in the passage above is the Hebrew word *elohim*. From the first word in Scripture we immediately see the main character come on to the scene. This main character acts upon the stage of eternity to do something only he can do – create. The Hebrew word *bara* describes God making everything in the beginning. This word is significant because it literally means to create something out of nothing. You and I can only make new things from older, preexisting things. Only God can create from nothing. Only he gets to *bara*.

---

[69] *Worthy are you, our Lord and God, to receive glory and honor and power, for you created all things, and by your will they existed and were created.* (Revelation 4:11)

Now, look closely at what we've just read. God made everything, and he made everything from nothing. How did he do that? With the word. When God wills to create everything, he speaks a Word. This powerful, preexistent word is how all things come into being. The Apostle John writes about this and says:

> *In the beginning was the Word, and the Word was with God, and the Word was God. He was in the beginning with God. All things were made through him, and without him was not any thing made that was made. In him was life, and the life was the light of men. The light shines in the darkness, and the darkness has not overcome it. The Word became flesh and dwelt among us... (John 1:1-5, 14).*

This is a stunning statement. Jesus, God's Son, the second person of the Trinity, is the Word through whom all things are made. He is the Word in Genesis. The one God speaks, and all things are made. So, through Christ, God the Father made everything, in the presence of the Spirit.

Look, there's the Trinity, right at the beginning.

Keep reading all of Genesis 1, and you'll see that the author goes to great lengths to express the goodness of God's handiwork. Seven times in the same chapter we're told that everything God made was good, as if to shout, "Pay attention! God's making something really great here!"

God makes light, and it's good. God makes dirt, and it's good. God makes plants, and they're good. God makes stars and planets whirling around the cosmos and – you guessed it – good. Then, to crown the creation over which God sang his song of creativity, God creates humans – beings capable of relationship with God himself and of stewarding all creation. God makes everything, literally everything, and it's very good (Gen. 1:31).

It's easy to allow the goodness of God's creation escape our notice. Watch the news for just a moment, and it's quite clear that we don't live in the world described in Genesis as "very good." In fact, the pristine goodness of creation only seems to last for a moment – two chapters, to be exact. But still we must see very clearly that when God created the world, it was without brokenness, without pain. It was full of justice and goodness. There were no tears of sadness, no broken relationships. It was good. The Hebrew language sums up the idea of the original state of creation in the word *shalom*. Shalom is often translated as "peace," but that's kind of the weak, diet-cola way to translate the word. Shalom means something much richer and fuller than simply the mere absence of conflict. When saying that God created the world in perfect shalom, what is meant is that everything was working as intended; in rhythm, beauty, life, and glory. It was like a tapestry – every part of creation woven over and under, beside and between every other part of creation, and all without conflict or friction. This interweaving of life and creation was so beautiful that when the Great Weaver stood back from his work, he saw it was very, very good. It was not just okay, it was the absolute best it has ever been.

According to John 1:1-3, who was "the Word" present in Genesis 1:1-3? What was that creation like?

Chapter Four – Origin

THE BIG REASON

Of course, all of this brings up still more questions. Namely, the question, "Why?" What purpose did God have in creating such a world?

The quest for "the meaning of life" has plagued humanity as long as we've been around. "Why am I here? What is my purpose?" Around my house, we like to start conversing about these questions early, so we loosely use the Catechism for Young Children. Its simple question-and-answer format makes it easy enough for even our littlest ones to remember. The first three questions, however, are of immediate relevance to us.

> Q. 1. Who made you?
> A. God.
>
> Q. 2. What else did God make?
> A. God made all things.
>
> Q. 3. Why did God make you and all things?
> A. For his own glory.

Simple, but profound. God made you and everything else, for his glory.

The glory of God is bound up in the purpose for creation itself. It's not incorrect to imagine the entire cosmos itself as a celestial cathedral given for the enjoyment and expansion of the glory of God, with all of humanity as its chief participant:

> So God created man in his own image, in the image of God he created him; male and female he
> created them. And God blessed them. And God said to them, "Be fruitful and multiply and fill the earth
> and subdue it, and have dominion over the fish of the sea and over the birds of the heavens and over
> every living thing that moves on the earth." (Genesis 1:27-28)

Humans were made to look like God! Not only that, but we were made to join in the creation family business. Making neighborhoods, gardens, and cities … we're invited to do it all with God, for the enjoyment of God's goodness – his glory.

Every field from medicine to music, science to social studies, plumbing to particle physics, can participate. No one is insignificant. No calling is second string. No job, no work, no area of study or standing in society is insignificant. You were made for the glory of God – to share it and to have your heart moved and your mind blown by it, so that in it, you would know God himself. God created the universe, matter, time, stars, planets, animals, and even you for one major, eternal purpose: to reflect and refract his glory.

Dr. John Piper connects the image of God in us with the glory of God, saying:

> He created us "in his image" so that we would image forth his glory in the world. We were made to be
> prisms refracting the light of God's glory into all of life. Why God should want to give us a share in shining

with his glory is a great mystery. Call it grace or mercy or love – it is an unspeakable wonder. Once we were not. Then we existed – for the glory of God![70]

Our lives are worth more than the mere sum of our accomplishments. Our destiny and future is greater than the shallows of physical pleasure. We were made to enjoy and display the glory of our Creator.

> *"The heavens declare the glory of God, and the sky above proclaims his handiwork. Day to day pours out speech, and night to night reveals knowledge,"* (Ps. 19:1-2).

> *"Bring my sons from afar and my daughters from the end of the earth, everyone who is called by my name, whom I created for my glory,"* (Is. 43:6b-7).

He made you in his image, to enjoy relationship with him. Glory.

> **Why did God make humans? How does this change the way you think of yourself and your vocation?**
> _____
> _____
> _____

THE BEGINNING OF BROKENNESS

God made the world good, yes. Yet, now it seems so very broken. How can we reconcile God's intentions with the brokenness we currently experience? It sure doesn't seem like the universe is echoing with the praises of the glory of God. What happened?

You can see brokenness all around you, can't you? When you walk down the street and see homelessness, poverty, and prostitution. When you turn on the news and hear of war, violence, rape, murder, and injustice. When you read about troops dying, cancer winning, and people hurting. When you look in the mirror and see the person starting back at you, far less than they should be. Some of you reading this need only reflect on the pain of your own upbringing – the abuse you've suffered, the loss you've experienced, and the pain you've endured.

How did it become this way?

---

[70] John Piper, *Desiring God.* (Colorado Springs, CO: Multnomah, 1986) 55.

Chapter Four – Origin

Our first parents were created to know and experience the greatness of God as persons. He formed them with his hands and breathed his very breath into their bodies to know them, be known by them.[71] They were his greatest work, his *magnum opus*, and they were to know him and oversee creation accordingly.[72] But, the command to go and take dominion included a warning. Should humanity seek to overthrow the rule of God, should his children choose to disconnect from the holy fusion of God and man, then it would all go very, very wrong for them.

> *You may surely eat of every tree of the garden, but of the tree of the knowledge of good and evil you shall not eat, for in the day that you eat of it you shall surely die... (Genesis 2:16-17).*

The tree represented something more – it symbolized a question: will humans trust God to define good and evil, right and wrong? Or, will they seize autonomy from God and define these things for themselves?

> *[The Serpent] said to the woman, "Did God actually say, 'You shall not eat of any tree in the garden'?" And the woman said to the serpent, "We may eat of the fruit of the trees in the garden, but God said, 'You shall not eat of the fruit of the tree that is in the midst of the garden, neither shall you touch it, lest you die.' " But the serpent said to the woman, "You will not surely die. For God knows that when you eat of it your eyes will be opened, and you will be like God, knowing good and evil." So when the woman saw that the tree was good for food, and that it was a delight to the eyes, and that the tree was to be desired to make one wise, she took of its fruit and ate, and she also gave some to her husband who was with her, and he ate. Then the eyes of both were opened, and they knew that they were naked. And they sewed fig leaves together and made themselves loincloths. (Genesis 3:1-7).*

The best kinds of lies always have a little bit of the truth in them. And indeed, it was a lie that duped our first parents into doing what they shouldn't have done. This mysterious character – evil embodied in a serpent – slithered up to Eve and began to whisper the seeds of doubt into her ears that fell like lead into her heart, "Did God actually say that you can't eat of any tree in the Garden?" (Gen. 3:1). A little bit of truth mingled with a lie. the question itself smacks of, "Poor you, God must be holding out on you ... "

Eve responds to correct the snake, but then gets a little mixed up.

> *We may eat of the fruit of the trees in the garden, but God said, 'You shall not eat of the fruit of the tree that is in the midst of the garden, neither shall you touch it, lest you die... (Genesis 3:2-3).*

That is almost what God said, but with an extra bit at the end. God simply said, "Do not eat." He did not say anything about touching. But, the seeds of doubt were sown. He saw his opening and he took it. His frontal assault followed, "you will not surely die. For God knows that when you eat of it ... you will be like God..."(Gen. 3:4-5).

To be like God.

Adam and Eve looked at the fruit and *decided for themselves* that it was good. Despite what God had explicitly told them, they trusted their reasons more than God's words. It was the first instance of human thought without respect to God's thought – the first moment that the creature presumed authority reserved for the Creator.

---

[71] Genesis 2:7

[72] Genesis 1:28-29

This was the first sin. Sin is any committed or omitted act, attitude, intention, or belief of the heart that is opposed to God. Sin shows itself in our desire to trust in ourselves, work for ourselves, focus on ourselves, and satisfy ourselves in ourselves, rather than God. At bottom, sin is rebellion on every level, because in it we decide to make everything about us and no longer fundamentally about God. In sinning, we turn the entire order of creation upside-down, and our not-so-subtle insurrection has dire cosmic consequences.

This was the great inversion that took place in the heart of God's children. The universe was made for God. In knowing and obeying God, humanity would have access to endless good, limitless joy, and unceasing peace. The fall inverted all of that – turned it upside down. In sin, our first parents desired life without God, and the great sadness is this: they got exactly what they wanted.

Of course, once you eject God from his creation, a few consequences follow. Remember what God told his children, "In the day you eat of it, you will surely die," (Gen. 2:17). So they took a bite … swallowed. They looked around and, what do you know, they weren't dead. Maybe they thought they'd gotten away with it. But what if God, in saying that death would come for sin, wasn't making an exaggerated threat, but a foreboding promise. Death for sin is more a factual statement of cause and effect than anything else. Think of this: if God is the source and author of all life, and in sinning we "unplug" our lives from God, then what is the result? A lack of life – and we commonly call that death. If you unplug your lamp from the wall you don't call the power company spiteful, you understand that lights simply don't work without electricity. So you're not surprised. Similarly, when life is unplugged from its source – as in the case of the fall – it's hardly surprising that death is the result.

Another implication of God's warning was that it wasn't for Adam and Eve alone. He was speaking to them and the humanity they represented.

> *"Therefore, just as sin came into the world through one man, and death through sin, and so death spread to all men because all sinned…"* (Romans 5:12)

That's the way sin is – it always affects people who had no choice in the matter. Like a cancer, sin attacks a small area first. But before long, the unaffected notice that they are hurting too. The cry of the autonomous heart is, "What does it matter to you what I do? I'm not hurting anyone else." But of course, you are. When you flourish, we flourish. When you fall, we get pulled down.

What is sin? How did it enter our world? How does it affect us?
_____
_____
_____

Chapter Four – Origin

THE SCOURGE OF SIN

In the first moments after rebellion, the unraveling effects of their treason began to take shape. Did they feel liberated? Free from God's oppressive rule? No. Nothing of the sort. Their first moments weren't the exhilaration of freedom from an oppressive master, as the liar had promised. No, the first feeling in their hearts was the same one we feel when we sin: shame. Michael Horton explains:

> *Adam's first sin was not in eating the forbidden fruit but in allowing the false witness to become a resident of the garden in the first place. The commission given to Adam and Eve above all else was to "work" and "keep" the sanctuary (Gen. 2:15; the same verbs used in the commission given to the priests in the Jerusalem temple). Instead of cleansing God's temple-garden as God's faithful servant and son, Adam entertained Satan himself and failed to protect Eve from his influence.*[73]

So, they did what we do when we feel shame – they hid. They ran from God. They saw their nakedness for the first time, and they were so disturbed that the only thing that they could think to do was to hide and cover up.

> *Then the eyes of both were opened, and they knew that they were naked. And they sewed fig leaves together and made themselves loincloths. And they heard the sound of the Lord God walking in the garden in the cool of the day, and the man and his wife hid themselves from the presence of the Lord God among the trees of the garden. But the Lord God called to the man and said to him, "Where are you?" And he said, "I heard the sound of you in the garden, and I was afraid, because I was naked, and I hid myself." He said, "Who told you that you were naked? Have you eaten of the tree of which I commanded you not to eat?" The man said, "The woman whom you gave to be with me, she gave me fruit of the tree, and I ate." Then the Lord God said to the woman, "What is this that you have done?" The woman said, "The serpent deceived me, and I ate…"* (Genesis 3:7-13).

Hiding. Blaming. Avoiding responsibility. The rest of Genesis 3 details the exact ways their preference for autonomy would now manifest itself, which can be summarized in at least four ways.

Fundamental	Relational	Creational	Personal
↑	↔	↓	→ ←
Our relationship with God is broken because of sin. (Is. 59:2)	Human relationships are now broken, due to sin. (Gen. 3)	Our relationship to the creation and our work therein is now cursed. (Gen 3:16-19)	Our relationship to ourselves is cursed, and now we hide and deceive ourselves. (Gen. 3:9-13)

---

[73] Horton, Michael S. (2011-01-04). *The Christian Faith: A Systematic Theology for Pilgrims on the Way* (Kindle Locations 10288-10291). Zondervan. Kindle Edition.

First, humanity's relationship to God was clearly now broken.[74] For, in deciding to become like God, they were effectively declaring war on their creator, saying, "We can do and be like you, so we don't need you anymore." This broken relationship became the source of all the other brokenness. Their sin had made a separation between them and God, and now God's presence would be hidden from them (Is. 59:2).[75]

Second, human relationships were now broken.[76] Since one human had decided to place herself in God's seat, the stage was set to invert the self-giving love of God into the self-seeking love of men. In seeking her own autonomy, Eve wasn't only saying that her desires were more important than God's, but also more important than anyone else's. Humanity would now no longer seek their greatest joy in the joy of others. Now, her progeny would seek their joy in themselves. You can probably see this in your own relationships: insecurity, codependency, abuse ... all of these are the fruits brought up from the root of selfishness.

Third, our relationship with the earth was tainted.[77] Before, Adam was set in the Garden as its master. He was told that he could simply eat of and enjoy the fruits of the Garden. But after sin, the Garden would no longer be for him but against him. It was as though the earth would rebel against its new rulers as it longed for the return of its true King.[78] The earth Adam would till would now fight him with thorns, thistles, and difficult labor all the days of his life. The very thing for which he was created would now war against him.

The curses of sin would not only flow outward, however. They would also rush inward. Humanity's deception was so dire that now even our ability to rightly understand ourselves was ruined. If we could manage to deceive ourselves into thinking that which was false was true, then we would no longer experience the mental and emotional perfection with which humans were made to live. Such is the inheritance of the inversion of sin; our very ability to know truth would no longer function properly. Theologians call this the noetic effect of sin – the inability to rightly interpret the information in the world around us. The result? Difference and strife over what is true and what is false, what is the right way to think and what is not.

How could the story possibly get better? Much of the rest of the Bible simply chronicles the way sin ruins everything. The effects are so devastating that Paul would later reflect:

> *None is righteous, no, not one; no one understands; no one seeks for God. All have turned aside; together they have become worthless; no one does good, not even one. Their throat is an open grave; they use their tongues to deceive. The venom of vipers is under their lips. Their mouth is full of curses and bitterness. Their feet are swift to shed blood; in their paths are ruin and misery, and the way of peace they have not*

---

[74] This can be seen in Adam and Eve's hiding from God and covering their nakedness, symbolizing a new barrier that existed between them and their Lord. Genesis 3:8

[75] This is summarized in the doctrine of total depravity. This sin nature, which all people now have by birth, is that capacity to do those things (good, neutral, or bad) which do not commend us to God. The Scriptures are filled with statements of the corruption of many aspects of man's nature. His intellect (2 Co 4:4; Ro 1:28), his conscience (1 Ti 4:2), his will (Ro 1:28), his heart (Eph 4:18), and his total being (Ro 1:18-3:20) have been corrupted. This is the doctrine of total depravity. Total depravity does not mean that everyone is as thoroughly depraved in his actions as he could possibly be, nor that everyone will indulge in every form of sin, nor that a person cannot appreciate and even do acts of goodness; but it does mean that the corruption of sin extends to all men and to all parts of all men so that there is nothing within the natural man that can give him merit in God's sight. (Ryrie, Charles Caldwell. *A Survey of Bible Doctrine*. Chicago: Moody Press, 1972.)

[76] A further implication of the coverings that Adam and Eve made for themselves is that they kept them from each other. Before, they were naked and unashamed, knowing each other and fully known by each other. Now, such intimacy was no longer possible. See Genesis 3:8, 16

[77] In Genesis 3:16-17, God curses the ground because of Adam's rebellion. This is very significant, because Adam's chiefest vocation was to tend, steward, manage, and bring food from the earth. Now, the very thing he was made to do would fight him.

[78] "For the creation waits with eager longing for the revealing of the sons of God." (Romans 8:19)

> known. There is no fear of God before their eyes. Therefore, just as sin came into the world through one man, and death through sin, and so death spread to all men because all sinned," (Romans 3:10-18; Romans 5:12).

What now of all that talk of imaging forth the glory of God into the world? What now of our purpose? The heart he formed was now cold to his touch. The ears he crafted, dead to his call. The soul he made to be satisfied in his presence, drinking deeply of the stagnant, waste water of this world.[79] Where once we were alive in God, we are now dead in sin – physically alive, spiritually dead.[80]

As a result of the fall, we sin because we are sinful. It's a part of who we are. And, we choose to confirm our nature quite frequently by doing what we ought not to do, or not doing what we should.

> All of us have become like one who is unclean, and all our righteous deeds are like a polluted garment; we all fade like a leaf, and our iniquities, like the wind, take us away. (Isaiah 64:6).

How broad are sin's effects? Read Ephesians 2:1-3.
_____
_____
_____

THERE'S A PROMISE IN THE PAIN

So, what hope do we have? So far in the story, humans are utterly lost – cut off from our God, the source of life and goodness, and there is nothing we are able to do about it. Considering all this, only one possible solution exists, a solution that comes from him and not us. Infinite gaps are not the types of things that finite beings are good at traversing. But, let's look at that passage in Genesis one more time.

Genesis 3 is an emotional passage. The angst of God's broken heart over his children's rebellion. The shame humans felt in the face of their Father. The seething rage and hatred of the tempter. The measured, righteous delivery of the sentence of death for treason. All of this is the kind of stuff which conjures up fear and sadness, not hope. And yet, deep within this painful passage, almost hidden in the curse of humanity's fallenness, there is a promise.

---

[79] "Be appalled, O heavens, at this; be shocked, be utterly desolate, declares the Lord, for my people have committed two evils: they have forsaken me, the fountain of living waters, and hewed out cisterns for themselves, broken cisterns that can hold no water." (Jeremiah 2:12-13)

[80] "And you were dead in the trespasses and sins in which you once walked, following the course of this world, following the prince of the power of the air, the spirit that is now at work in the sons of disobedience – among whom we all once lived in the passions of our flesh, carrying out the desires of the body and the mind, and were by nature children of wrath, like the rest of mankind." (Ephesians 2:1-3)

The Lord God said to the serpent ... "I will put enmity between you and the woman, and between your offspring and her offspring; he shall bruise your head, and you shall bruise his heel," (Genesis 3:14-15).

There is God, speaking to the liar himself – the one who sowed the seeds of doubt into the heart of humanity. God makes him a promise: though he tried to destroy our first mother, there will be one who comes from her who will destroy *him*. Our enemy will try to hurt this rescuing son, but in doing so he will be crushed under the weight of this promised rescuer. Somewhere, somehow, God will orchestrate the story which follows on from this moment to bring about a victory over our enemy. The curse of sin brought with it a promise – a promise of rescue.

Here we see exactly what kind of God we're getting to know. He's not the kind of God who hits the reset button. He doesn't abandon his kids like a bad father who gets upset at the family and walks out. He's the kind of dad who promises that no matter what it costs, how long it takes, how much it hurts, or what kinds of chasms must be crossed, rescue is coming.

And come it does.

APPLICATION & REFLECTION

1. According to this chapter, why did God make you and everything else? Why is the glory of God good news?

2. According to Genesis 1:26-28, what job did God give the first people? Read 1 Corinthians 10:31. What might it look like for you to obey this verse?

3. Briefly summarize the false views of naturalism and pantheism. How is Christianity different than these views? Why are these views bad explanations of the world?

4. Are God and creation the same thing? Why not? How did God make the world?

5. Why doesn't evolution disprove the doctrine of creation?

Origin – **Chapter Four**

6. What is sin? Read Genesis 3:7-10. How did Adam and Eve react when they realized they sinned? Why? What did God do in verse 8-9?

   _____
   _____
   _____

7. How does Ephesians 2:13 describe all of us? Can we seek God in such a condition?

   _____
   _____
   _____

8. How does Isaiah 64:6 describe even the best efforts made by sinful people? According to Isaiah 59:1-2, what does our sin do to our relationship with God?

   _____
   _____
   _____

9. Read Romans 3:1-20. Describe our sinful condition characterized in this passage. Can we seek God and mend the gap on our own?

   _____
   _____

10. Read Romans 3:10-18. How does this passage describe us apart from God's grace?

    _____
    _____

SCRIPTURE

Genesis 1-3	Isaiah 40:28	Colossians 1:16
Hebrews 11:3	1 Corinthians 8:6	Revelation 4:11
Isaiah 43:6b-7	Romans 1:18-3:20, 5:12-21	Ephesians 2:1-3

Chapter Four – Origin

CHAPTER FIVE

REDEMPTION

Chapter Five – Redemption

AFTER THE FALL

After creation, God's rescue plan began. Everything after this moment would be saturated with both the pain of sin and the promise of redemption. Somewhere around seventh grade English class you probably learned about foreshadowing. Any good novel uses foreshadowing to draw the reader's attention above the events that are happening on the page and into the possible events which await them on the pages to come. It's a way to build dramatic tension which culminates when the story turns, the conflict is resolved, the hero wins, and the enemy is defeated. And this story is full of redemptive foreshadowing.

Our greatest stories have great heroes. Why is that? It's because *the* story – the gospel story – is like that. The one, overarching narrative of the Scriptures is the story of God's great rescue of the people he loves. And it starts with skins:

> *And the Lord God made for Adam and for his wife garments of skins and clothed them. Then the Lord God said, "Behold, the man has become like one of us in knowing good and evil. Now, lest he reach out his hand and take also of the tree of life and eat, and live forever–" therefore the Lord God sent him out from the garden of Eden to work the ground from which he was taken.* (Genesis 3:21-23).

The fig leaves they put on weren't enough – an inadequate solution for their problem. So, God took skin and covered the shame and the reproach of his children. You don't have to be a zoologist to know what had to happen prior to God putting clothes on Adam and Eve. Animals don't willingly give up their skin. An innocent creature had to be sacrificed to cover the guilty. The wages of sin is death (Rom. 6:23), so in these clothes – these skins – we see the cost for covering sin. For humanity's shame to be covered, blood had to be shed. In his love, God deflected this off of the children he loved on to an innocent creature which gave its life for them. Because of his love, God would not allow his children to perpetually exist in a state of sinfulness. He removed them so that he could rescue them

Right there at the crime scene of the cosmos, God showed mercy to humanity at the expense of an innocent creature. The world after the fall – the world in which we live – is the world of depravity. *Total* depravity. Brokenness and sin sickness are everywhere, and no one is immune. And yet there God is, showing love and mercy to his people.

My main goal in this chapter is to give you new glasses through which to read the Scriptures, glasses that see the overarching, loving, redemptive, covenantal purposes of God to reconcile the world to himself. To do this, I want to highlight four major moments in the story. These are not the only moments, but they serve to illustrate very well the kind of God we're talking about. They are the stories of Noah, Abraham, Moses and the Day of Atonement, and finally, the life of Jesus himself. In each of these stories we'll see how it was God's mercy, his love, his initiation, and his power which rescued his people.

How did God respond to Adam and Eve's sinful rebellion? What does this teach you about God?

_____
_____
_____

Redemption – **Chapter Five**

THE (FIRST) SAVIOR OF THE WORLD

Like a flooding river, the sinfulness of humanity after the fall eventually overran the world. From Genesis 3 to 6, humanity goes on a downward spiral, with tragic story after tragic story which led God to feel the kind of sadness in his heart that only comes from a father whose children are wayward.[81] Everything and everyone was only doing evil all the time. And yet, he showed mercy to a man named Noah.

Now, if you went to Sunday school like I did, then you learned why this happened. I remember it as though it were yesterday. The sweet lady in the long dress explained that Noah was rescued by God because he was a righteous man. Of all the people on Earth, only Noah was God's follower and friend. And that's true, Noah was singularly righteous in a generation of wickedness. But, is that why he was chosen? Let's read the story.

> *The Lord saw that the wickedness of man was great in the earth, and that every intention of the thoughts of his heart was only evil continually. And the Lord regretted that he had made man on the earth, and it grieved him to his heart. So the Lord said, "I will blot out man whom I have created from the face of the land, man and animals and creeping things and birds of the heavens, for I am sorry that I have made them." But Noah found favor in the eyes of the Lord.* (Genesis 6:5-8).

Did you catch it? Look at the order there.

1. The Lord saw everyone was wicked and evil only and always. (v. 5)

2. The Lord decided to "blot out man," which is a polite, biblical euphemism for destroying everyone and everything. (v. 7)

3. Noah found "favor" with God. (v. 8)

God was so saddened and righteously indignant with the state of his creation that he was prepared to destroy everyone and everything in it. Rather than allow humanity to continue in its downward spiral, God would literally wash it all away. But then, Noah found favor in the eyes of the Lord.

Now, wait a minute. I thought that everyone everywhere was only doing evil all the time? Is this passage teaching us that God was about to smash everything to bits but then at the last minute he was distracted by one man who was living righteously? How could Noah have been so righteous that God saved him, if everyone everywhere was only and always evil? Well, maybe everyone was evil and broken but Noah, right?

Wrong.

That's not what the Scriptures say. In fact, it's not even what they suggest. The Bible is clear. *Everyone* was evil, and God's right response to such depravity was to wipe it out. But that leaves us with one burning question, then. How did Noah find favor?

---

[81] *And the Lord regretted that he had made man on the earth, and it grieved him to his heart.* (Genesis 6:6)

Chapter Five – Redemption

The answer is there in the text. The word here is the Hebrew word *chen* (חֵן), which translates to "favor, grace."[82] Noah didn't have a sudden change of heart. Noah wasn't searching for something called "favor" and found it. Instead, the word gives us a picture of a redeeming Father looking down at his creation who all deserved nothing but judgment for their treasonous abandonment of God, and instead decided to show favor to this man and his family, in order that generations after him might be rescued. Kurt Strassner explains:

> *Reading those verses, we could now launch into a nice "be like Noah" sermon – like those that many of us heard as children. But that is not the point of the passage. The thrust of this chapter is not that Noah was good, but that God is gracious. Look closely at verse 8: "Noah found favor in the eyes of the Lord." The word translated "favor" here is the Hebrew word that means "grace." Noah found grace – free, unmerited kindness – in the eyes of the Lord. Noah was righteous and blameless, yes. But he wasn't naturally so. By nature, Noah was a born sinner – just look at him sprawled out drunk and naked on his living room floor at the end of chapter 9! The curse of Adam had fallen as heavily on Noah as it had on anyone else. So the only reason Noah was "blameless in his time" was because God had shown him "favor!"*[83]

This is a critical point we can't miss – *God* saved Noah. God's love for Noah overcame Noah's natural rebellion, and his whole family was saved. Think of what this meant for Noah. Encountering God's favor didn't only mean being saved himself. God gave Noah a new mission – to be the vessel of rescue for others. This meant Noah embarking on a very long project of building, along with his sons, an ark. It meant work, preparation, and probably quite a few strange looks from the neighbors at the man who built a ship in the middle of the desert.

And now, you're here to read this book. Good thing God showed Noah grace.

Was Noah perfect? No. Noah still had many warts, flaws, and issues. I mean, let's not forget that he decided to celebrate his great and mighty salvation from the Lord with a binge-drinking party that landed him naked and wasted in his tent.[84] However, God was pleased to use this broken man to show his saving, redeeming love. He saved him and helped him, despite him, because he loved him.

> *...whoever would draw near to God must believe that he exists and that he rewards those who seek him. By faith Noah, being warned by God concerning events as yet unseen, in reverent fear constructed an ark for the saving of his household.* (Hebrews 11:6-7)

According to the Noah story above, why did God save him?
___
___
___

---

[82] Robert L. Thomas, *New American Standard Hebrew-Aramaic and Greek Dictionaries : Updated Edition*, G1. Anaheim: Foundation Publications, Inc., 1998.

[83] Strassner, Kurt. *Opening Up Genesis*. Opening Up Commentary. Leominster: Day One Publications, 2009.

[84] Genesis 9:21

FATHER ABRAHAM

A few chapters after Noah we meet a man named Abram. By all accounts, Abram was a nominally religious, fairly successful man, looking forward to enjoying a happy retirement in the not-too-distant future. He lived in Ur, a thriving town of the time. Yet, God came to this otherwise unexceptional man and said, "Follow me to a land that you've never been to before, and I will bless you and your offspring, and make you a blessing to the world."[85]

What?

What had Abram done to deserve such a blessing? Like Noah, nothing. In fact, Abram had done a few things that you'd think would *disqualify* him from usefulness to God. He was from an idolatrous, pagan city. Prior to his encounter with God, he likely worshipped the moon like everyone else in his hometown.[86] Later in his life, he'll put his wife in harm's way to save himself. Abram, like Noah, wasn't short on personal issues.

And, that's precisely the point: God's never-stopping love had found another recipient in Abram. Was he deserving of God's blessing? No. No one ever is. His problems were Noah's problems, and their problems were Adam's. Yet, Abram is often remembered for what he did next, which was to simply and unquestioningly follow God wherever he led. The word for this is *faith*.

Such faith is exemplary, and certainly worth imitating. But, this man of faith never earned the promises he believed. He couldn't! God came to him in the midst of his comfortable near-retirement life and called him, undeserving though he was. Abram wasn't a religious seeker, looking to encounter God. We have no reason to believe that he was somehow unfulfilled or searching for higher meaning in the universe. If anything, it seems like he had every reason to stay right where he was. God simply and sovereignly appears to this man, by grace, and everything changes.

> *Now the Lord said to Abram, "Go from your country and your kindred and your father's house to the land that I will show you. And I will make of you a great nation, and I will bless you and make your name great, so that you will be a blessing. I will bless those who bless you, and him who dishonors you I will curse, and in you all the families of the earth shall be blessed." So Abram went, as the Lord had told him...* (Genesis 12:1-4).

Suddenly, unexpectedly, God speaks. Abram obeys. He would bless Abram so that he might be a blessing.

Again, we see the pattern set by God in Genesis 3. God acts graciously toward a man who didn't deserve it. He covers his sin and makes a great promise, all the while using this man and his family as vessels through which God's relentless love might flow to the world. Biblical scholar Michael Goheen summarizes this point well, saying:

> *When human disobedience defiles all creation (including all human culture), God immediately promises that he will crush all the evil forces unleashed by Adam and Eve's rebellion (Gen. 3:15). God sets out on a*

---

[85] Genesis 12:1-3

[86] The Sumerian god *Sin* was worshipped in Ur.

Chapter Five – Redemption

long journey of restoration, maintaining his promise to heal creation in spite of persistent human failure and faithlessness. The election of Abraham and God's promise to make him a great nation need to be understood within this overarching narrative framework: God intends that the entire creation and all human life and culture might through Abraham become "very good" once again ... God is still pursuing the restoration of creation [and] will now do so ... through Abraham.[87]

The calling of Abraham established the people of Israel, who will eventually come from this one man. This people is formed from the unlikeliest of sources – an old man married to a woman who can't have children. God was creating a people to know him uniquely, and through them invite the world to know him as well. Just as Abraham was saved by grace through faith in God's promise to bless the world, so now Israel will carry that promise forward. Israel was to be the means by which God accomplished the goal of renewing all nations and all creation.

> **Read Genesis 15:16 and Galatians 3:5-7. How was Abraham justified?**
> _____
> _____
> _____

THE DAY OF ATONEMENT

So far we've seen this pattern: God calls and rescues, his people respond with faith and obedience, and through them God accomplishes a victory. Yet, their sinfulness continues to be a problem.

Unfortunately, the root of sinfulness isn't a surface root, easily killed by striking the visible fruit. Sin's roots are buried far below the soil of behavior, beneath the dirt of emotions; the root of sin is wrapped around the very bedrock of human identity – the heart. How would God reach deep enough to uproot sin without killing the fragile sapling of humanity?

Fast-forwarding a few centuries after Abraham, we come to the life of a man named Moses. Moses was a semi-orphaned Israelite, saved from an early death by the quick thinking of his mother. The king of Egypt, after decreeing that all young male Israelite children should be killed, sent his soldiers to carry out mass infanticide. But Moses' mother hid her son in a basket in the Nile River, far from harm. Upon being found by one of the princesses of the kingdom, he was adopted into the king's family and was raised in the palace. Learning later of his Israelite heritage, Moses began to identify with his people, leading him to murder a solider for mistreating an Israelite slave. To flee punishment for his crime, Moses left Egypt for the deserts of Midian.

But God had a plan for Moses. In the midst of his exile and wandering in Midian, God spoke to him. That fact alone is worth noting for the simple reason that he, like all our other characters, had nothing on his resumé to merit a relationship with God.

---

[87] Michael Goheen, *A Light to the Nations.* (Grand Rapids, MI: Baker Academic, 2011) 28.

He was a murderer and a traitor to his own people, living in luxury in the palace while they lived in oppression in the fields. He wasn't all that skilled, either. He himself confessed to being a poor communicator and a bad leader. And, that is precisely the point. God calls Moses and invites him to participate in his plan of redemption, all as a result of God's grace and not owing at all to Moses' skills.

God meant for his redemption project to continue, and that meant the captivity of God's people had to be overcome. Moses was living in a time when Abraham's children – Israel – were, as an entire nation, living as slaves in Egypt. For four hundred years God's people had been in captivity, wondering where the promises of God's redeeming love had gone. Much to their surprise, he was again calling a very unlikely individual to play a critical role in their redemption.

Moses, the traitor-prince turned wandering shepherd, would now embrace God's call. He returned to Egypt and commanded Pharaoh to release God's people. After 10 plagues, the people in slavery were led by Moses to freedom. This deliverance was punctuated by amazing nature-miracles, where the God of creation flexed his divine muscle over the world (like when a few million of his people were led across dry land because God split the sea in half, and then closed it back on top of their enemies).

Adam and Eve	Noah	Abraham	Moses
Fallen in Sin "Behold, the man knows ... evil." (Gen 3:22)	**Fallen in Sin** "...the wickedness of man was great, and every intention of his heart was only evil..." (Gen 6:5)	**Fallen in Sin** Abraham was from Ur, a pagan city. (Gen 11:27-30)	**Fallen in Sin** Moses was a murderer and convict on the run. (Ex 2:11-15)
Shown Grace by God "So God made for [them] garments of skins and clothed them." (Gen 3:20)	**Shown Grace by God** "But Noah found favor (grace) in the eyes of the Lord" (Gen 6:8)	**Shown Grace by God** "The Lord said ... I will make you a great nation and I will bless you..." (Gen 12:2)	**Shown Grace by God** "...the Angel of the Lord appeared to Moses in a flame..." (Ex 3:2)
Respond in Faith Go out from the garden into the world. (Gen 4)	**Respond in Faith** Builds the ark. (Gen 7)	**Respond in Faith** Believes God and it's counted to him as righteousness. (Gen 15:6)	**Respond in Faith** Goes to Pharoah. (Ex 6)
Brought into God's Redemptive Plan "He will crush your head, you shall bruise his heel..." (Gen 3:15) "Now Adam knew his wife Eve and they conceived..." (Gen 4:1)	**Brought into God's Redemptive Plan** "Go into the ark..." (Gen 7:1)	**Brought into God's Redemptive Plan** Abraham became the father of the faith. "I will bless you ... so that you will be a blessing ... In you all the families of the Earth shall be blessed." (Gen 12:3)	**Brought into God's Redemptive Plan** Moses was the first great leader of God's people. "I will send you to Pharoah..." (Ex 3:10)

The chart above shows how we've seen God redeem his people so far.

After a history lesson like that, you'd think that God's people would be chomping at the bit to obey him out of thankfulness. But we are all too familiar with our own hearts to know that such a response would never actually happen. God rescued his people. God redeemed them. God saved them. God fed them. God protected them. God led them. And yet, most of the history of this period is littered with their constant complaining, disobedience, whining, and waywardness. It's like the parents who take their kids to Disney World, thinking that out of sheer gratitude and loving thankfulness they'll be on their best behavior, only to find

Chapter Five – Redemption

them arguing over their $15 Mickey Mouse Popsicle inside the Magic Kingdom. The heart of man is still broken, even in the happiest place on earth.

So, how was God to deal with this? For an answer, let's examine something called *The Day of Atonement*.

After God's people were freed from slavery, God gave them laws by which they should live as his people. They were to be his people and he their God. For a moment at least, it looked like the story of redemption was coming to a close. Perhaps the longed-for happy ending was near. But it wasn't. God's people couldn't obey. But of course, God knew that too. He also instituted a system of sacrifices for sin – a reminder that the results of sin are always death. Note the pattern: God called Moses, rescued Israel, and then gave them the law. Call, redemption, instruction.

Just as an animal had to die to cover Adam and Eve, blood was needed again to cover sin. The right payment for sin was death, because sin was the undoing of God's creation, the rejection of God – the Author of Life.

It was about this very situation that God spoke to Moses and established this solemn, special day.[88] Once a year, Israel would come to The Day of Atonement (*Yom Kippur*). On this day, the priest would take two spotless goats, the best of the flock. Over one goat, the priest would confess all the sins of the people. You can imagine that this might take quite some time, as the mediator between God and his people would painstakingly review all the ways that God's people had failed to live up to their end of the covenant. Finally, when confession was done, the severity of sin would be exemplified for all to see as the priest slaughtered the animal – the blood of the substitute covering the guilty. Something had died the death they deserved, so that they didn't have to.

Then came the second part of the ritual. After the priest had washed himself, he would return and take with him the second of the two goats. Again, he would confess the sins of the people over this animal. But this time, the innocent animal was led outside the city and sent away, never to return. Bearing the sins of the people, this creature would be cast out – a picture of the sins of God's people being taken away. Two animals, two fates, one picture of redemption.

> **The story of Israel is a complicated history of human rebellion and divine love. How does this overview help you understand God's heart to save his people?**
> _____
> _____
> _____

---

[88] For a complete description of the Day of Atonement, see Leviticus 16

UNRESOLVED TENSION

These stories, and hundreds of others in the Old Testament, leave the reader with at least two distinct impressions. We're first struck by God's love – the kind of love that chases down men like Noah, Abram, and Moses. God rescues them, despite them, for him. Yet, we're also struck by the price of usurping God's authority, and the death which has been unleashed because of sin.

God would frequently send messengers called prophets to highlight this tension. These men of God would roam the kingdom preaching the doom and gloom of judgment right alongside the sweet promises of redeeming love. Some prophets were loved and honored, but many were ignored, or worse. Because God's people wouldn't listen, they were eventually carried off into slavery, losing the nation that God gave them. Men like Jeremiah, who lived long after all the promises to Moses and Abraham would be inspired to proclaim:

> *Behold, the days are coming, declares the LORD, when I will make a new covenant with the house of Israel and the house of Judah, not like the covenant that I made with their fathers on the day when I took them by the hand to bring them out of the land of Egypt, my covenant that they broke, though I was their husband, declares the LORD. For this is the covenant that I will make with the house of Israel after those days, declares the LORD: I will put my law within them, and I will write it on their hearts. And I will be their God, and they shall be my people. And no longer shall each one teach his neighbor and each his brother, saying, 'Know the LORD,' for they shall all know me, from the least of them to the greatest, declares the LORD. For I will forgive their iniquity, and I will remember their sin no more, (Jeremiah 31:31-34).*

Write his law on their hearts? Everyone will know him? How?

Isaiah would describe the hoped-for king – the Messiah – in these ways:

> *For to us a child is born, to us a son is given; and the government shall be upon his shoulder, and his name shall be called Wonderful Counselor, Mighty God, Everlasting Father, Prince of Peace. Of the increase of his government and of peace there will be no end, on the throne of David and over his kingdom, to establish it and to uphold it with justice and with righteousness from this time forth and forevermore. The zeal of the Lord of hosts will do this. (Isaiah 9:6-7).*

> *Behold my servant, whom I uphold, my chosen, in whom my soul delights; I have put my Spirit upon him; he will bring forth justice to the nations. He will not cry aloud or lift up his voice, or make it heard in the street; a bruised reed he will not break, and a faintly burning wick he will not quench; he will faithfully bring forth justice. (Is 42:1-3).*

Repeatedly conquered, divided, and overrun with false worship, the picture becomes clear: if the gulf between God and his people is to be crossed, then God must be the one to traverse it. Things in Israel had gone beyond all repair, all hope. Yet, in the darkness of their situation, the words of the prophet Isaiah echoed:

> *For behold, darkness shall cover the earth, and thick darkness the peoples; But the Lord will rise upon you, and his glory will be seen upon you. And nations shall come to your light, and kings to the brightness of your rising. (Isaiah 60:2-3)*

Chapter Five – Redemption

Strangely, after all these prophetic books, the Old Testament simply ends. God loves his people, God hates sin and what it does to the world. Where's it all going? Who is this messiah, and when will he arrive?

> **Read Isaiah 52:13 - 53:12. How does this prophetic poem, written hundreds of years before Jesus, shape your understanding of Messiah, and how God would resolve the tension of his love and justice?**
>
> _____
> _____
> _____

JESUS CHRIST

Almost 400 years passed between the last prophet of Israel and the birth of Jesus Christ. That's a long time for this unresolved tension to exist. But, like any good piece of music, theater, or poetry, the more dramatic the tension, the greater the resolution. And, the resolution that was coming would be glorious.

For these four centuries the hope of this promise – "I will be their God and they shall be my people" – went unseen. Yet this dramatic collision between divinity and humanity occurred in the most un-dramatic of ways: the birth of a baby in a backwater town on the edge of the Roman empire.

> *In the beginning was the Word, and the Word was with God, and the Word was God. He was in the beginning with God. All things were made through him, and without him was not any thing made that was made. In him was life, and the life was the light of men. The light shines in the darkness, and the darkness has not overcome it. The true light, which gives light to everyone, was coming into the world. He was in the world, and the world was made through him, yet the world did not know him. He came to his own, and his own people did not receive him. But to all who did receive him, who believed in his name, he gave the right to become children of God, who were born, not of blood nor of the will of the flesh nor of the will of man, but of God. And the Word became flesh and dwelt among us, and we have seen his glory, glory as of the only Son from the Father, full of grace and truth. John bore witness about him, and cried out, "This was he of whom I said, 'He who comes after me ranks before me, because he was before me.'" For from his fullness we have all received, grace upon grace. For the law was given through Moses; grace and truth came through Jesus Christ. No one has ever seen God; the only God, who is at the Father's side, he has made him known, (John 1:1-5, 9-18).*

This is unimaginably good news. The promised rescuer, the seed of the woman, the blessing of the nations, love of God and the deliverer of justice – that One – has finally come.

God's promise of a rescuer that would crush the tempter, a salvation greater than the ark of Noah, a promise better than Abraham imagined, and an inheritance more perfect than Moses dreamed, was coming true.

Jesus is the great king who would come to put away sin, and resolve the tension of God's love for his people and his commitment to act justly for the world. Consider how Paul reflects on this:

> *For while we were still weak, at the right time Christ died for the ungodly. For one will scarcely die for a righteous person—though perhaps for a good person one would dare even to die – but* **God shows his love** *for us in that while we were still sinners, Christ died for us. Since, therefore,* **we have now been justified** *by his blood, much more shall we be saved by him from the wrath of God.* (Romans 5:6-9, emphasis mine).

Everybody of every religion wants a piece of Jesus. For the Muslims, he's the precursor prophet to Muhammed. For the Hindus, he's a holy god-man in the pantheon of millions of others. For the eastern mystics, he's a philosopher deeply attuned to the universe. For the Western skeptic, he's a good teacher of ethical principles. But who is Jesus?

It's popular to compliment Jesus while denying his divinity. Doing so makes us feel like we've tipped our hat to a good man, but not gone along with the crazy assumption that he was anything more. But, when we do this, we're not tipping our hat to Jesus. We're tipping our hat to someone else entirely. Jesus went about telling people that he was God, and the Son of God.[89] He added to that claim a host of others, most remarkable among which is the claim that without faith in him, no one can know God (Jn. 14:6). To call Jesus a prophet sounds nice to say, but doing so reveals more about one's ignorance of the historical record than it does an affinity for Jesus. Good prophets don't tell people they're God. Nice teachers don't get murdered. Moral men don't make claims to divinity. C.S. Lewis made a similar point long ago:

> *I am trying here to prevent anyone saying the really foolish thing that people often say about him: I'm ready to accept Jesus as a great moral teacher, but I don't accept his claim to be God. That is the one thing we must not say. A man who was merely a man and said the sort of things Jesus said would not be a great moral teacher. He would either be a lunatic – on the level with the man who says he is a poached egg – or else he would be the Devil of Hell. You must make your choice. Either this man was, and is, the Son of God, or else a madman or something worse. You can shut him up for a fool, you can spit at him and kill him as a demon or you can fall at his feet and call him Lord and God, but let us not come with any patronizing nonsense about his being a great human teacher. He has not left that open to us. He did not intend to. ... Now it seems to me obvious that he was neither a lunatic nor a fiend: and consequently, however strange or terrifying or unlikely it may seem, I have to accept the view that he was and is God."*[90]

This is the shocking claim: God's promise throughout the history of redemption came true in his son, Jesus Christ. His incarnation is the culmination of prophecy, foreshadow, and promise. Complimenting Jesus' ethics or spirituality while denying his divinity is like complimenting the firefighter on his hat as you kick him out of your blazing home. The arrival of Jesus Christ as something altogether more transformational than our quaint, patronizing categories. His arrival inaugurated the kingdom of God, and God the Son was bringing it.

> *Jesus came into Galilee, proclaiming the gospel of God, and saying, "The time is fulfilled, and the kingdom of God is at hand; repent and believe in the gospel." (Mark 1:14-15).*

---

[89] See Matt. 27:43, Luke 22:70, John 3:18, 10:36, 11:4, 27, et. al.

[90] C.S. Lewis, *Mere Christianity*, (London: Collins, 1952) 54-56.

Chapter Five – Redemption

> **According to C.S. Lewis, why is it impossible to relegate Jesus to the status of "good teacher?"**
> _____
> _____
> _____

THE LIFE OF JESUS

Some attempt to make sense of Jesus by only examining his life – the teaching, the miracles, etc. Others say, "No, the main thing about Jesus was his death." Still others reject both of these approaches and try to see him only in the light of the resurrection. But, to understand Jesus, we must see all of him – his life, death, and resurrection. So, let's start with his life.

Jesus' life on earth was preceded by a striking amount of prophecy. Countless types, foreshadowings, and fore-tellings occur all throughout the Bible for one purpose: so we'll know him when we see him. Isaiah tells us that, "the Lord himself will give [us] a sign: the virgin will be with child and will give birth to a son, and will call him Immanuel" (Isaiah 7:14). Concerning the ministry of this rescuer who would be born of a virgin, he writes:

> *He was despised and rejected by men; a man of sorrows, and acquainted with grief; and as one from whom men hide their faces, he was despised, and we esteemed him not. Surely he has borne our griefs and carried our sorrows; yet we esteemed him stricken, smitten by God, and afflicted. But he was pierced for our transgressions; he was crushed for our iniquities; upon him was the chastisement that brought us peace, and with his wounds we are healed. All we like sheep have gone astray; we have turned – every one – to his own way; and the LORD has laid on him the iniquity of us all.* (Isaiah 53:3-6).

Consider this:

- In Genesis, Jesus is the powerful Word of creation (Gen. 1:1)
- Jesus is the offspring of the woman who would defeat God's enemy (Gen. 3:15).
- In Exodus, he's the truer redeemer of the greater Israel – all of God's people – taking us from slavery to sin into the promised land of salvation. The promise of forgiveness for sin causes the reader to look forward to Christ who would give himself as the true sacrifice for sin (Rom. 8:3).
- In the history of the kings of Israel we look forward to Christ, the true King who will rule with all justice and power. After the capture and captivity of Israel, the restoration of true worship is figurative of Christ, the one who restores us to true worship of God (Ez. 3:2).

Not only does Jesus fulfill every scriptural expectation, he repeatedly demonstrated the kind of power and authority that backed up his claim to be the Son of God. When he spoke to the men of the day, they answered him and obeyed him like

God.[91] Can you imagine the kind of gravitas such a man must have had, to tell a gang of gruff young men to follow him? He wasn't the pretty man surrounded by cute, fluffy sheep in your grandmother's painting. This was a man with authority.

There was something about him that went beyond eloquence and charisma. Mark notes that "They were astonished at his teaching, for he taught them as one who had authority, and not as the scribes," (Mark 1:22). This authority extended into the real world. When he prayed, sick people become well,[92] and dead people returned to life.[93] It was as though he, the Word of God present at the moment of creation, was calling out to the world he made, and the atoms, the seas, the cells ... they all obeyed him. Creation responding to the voice of its creator – as if the Kingdom long without its King remembered his voice from an age long past, and obeyed.

He fulfilled prophecy. He taught with authority. He healed the sick. He raised the dead. He defied expectations He spoke the very words of God.

What stands out to you about the life of Jesus that makes him more than a mere religious teacher?
___
___
___

THE DEATH OF JESUS

The cross of Jesus Christ is central to the Christian story. This one act – the death of the Son of God for sinners – simultaneously reveals the pinnacle of God's love and the depth of humanity's sin. But, why did this happen? If death is the inheritance that sin – the unhitching of life from the life-giver – provides, then there are at least three good reasons that Jesus Christ had to die: to absorb the wrath of God in our place, to reconcile us to God and each other, and to demonstrate his amazing love.

---

[91] *Passing alongside the Sea of Galilee, he saw Simon and Andrew the brother of Simon casting a net into the sea, for they were fishermen. And Jesus said to them, "Follow me, and I will make you become fishers of men." And immediately they left their nets and followed him.* (Mark 1:16-18)

[92] *That evening at sundown they brought to him all who were sick or oppressed by demons. And the whole city was gathered together at the door. And he healed many who were sick with various diseases, and cast out many demons.* (Mark 1:32-34)

[93] *And when the Lord saw her, he had compassion on her and said to her, "Do not weep." Then he came up and touched the bier, and the bearers stood still. And he said, "Young man, I say to you, arise." And the dead man sat up and began to speak, and Jesus gave him to his mother.* (Luke 7:13-15)

Chapter Five – Redemption

Only thinking about Jesus' life leads to an anemic, "Jesus was a really good person, so you go be good too," gospel. While mercy and acts of kindness are crucial, they cannot be alone. After all, Jesus spent a lot of life teaching about his death.[94] So critical is his death that in the book of Revelation Jesus is called, "the lamb of God slain before the foundations of the world." Don't miss that. The book called "The Revelation of Jesus Christ," reveals him as the one who came to die – a plan enacted before creation even began.

This is Jesus. The blood of God himself, spilled for humanity.

> *But as it is, he has appeared once for all at the end of the ages to put away sin by the sacrifice of himself* (Hebrews 9:26).

Speaking of the amazing wonder of this sacrifice, John Piper says, "the death of Christ is the wisdom of God by which the love of God saves sinners from the wrath of God, and all the while upholds and demonstrates the righteousness of God."[95]

> *You were ransomed from the futile ways inherited from your forefathers, not with perishable things such as silver or gold, but with the precious blood of Christ, like that of a lamb without blemish or spot.*
> (1 Peter 1:18-19).

Can you hear the resolution to the tension? Do you see the story coming together? On the cross, the love of God meets the wrath of God in the death of the Son of God for the people of God. Here in the cross we find the resolution – the glorious, scandalous, beautiful, and terrible resolution to the tension of the entirety of redemptive history up to this point, and the sound is an awe-full and wonderful one.

Jesus' death resolves the dissonance of our treasonous rebellion against God and God's relentless love for us. In the death of the Son of God, God takes sin seriously enough to do something about it while being merciful – pouring his wrath out on someone else so that he could save his people. Justice and mercy met where blood and water flowed.

Here, I think it most appropriate to let the Scriptures speak for themselves.

> *For all have sinned and fall short of the glory of God, and are justified by his grace as a gift, through the redemption that is in Christ Jesus, whom God put forward as a propitiation by his blood, to be received by faith. This was to show God's righteousness, because in his divine forbearance he had passed over former sins. It was to show his righteousness at the present time, so that he might be just and the justifier of the one who has faith in Jesus* (Romans 3:23-26).

> *For our sake he made him to be sin who knew no sin, so that in him we might become the righteousness of God* (2 Corinthians 5:21).

> *He himself bore our sins in his body on the tree, that we might die to sin and live to righteousness. By his wounds you have been healed* (1 Peter 2:24).

---

[94] See John 11:13, 18:32

[95] John Piper, *Desiring God*. Colorado Springs, CO: Multnomah. 1986, 60.

> *Yet it was the will of the LORD to crush him; he has put him to grief; when his soul makes an offering for guilt, he shall see his offspring; he shall prolong his days; the will of the LORD shall prosper in his hand. Out of the anguish of his soul he shall see and be satisfied; by his knowledge shall the righteous one, my servant, make many to be accounted righteous, and he shall bear their iniquities* (Isaiah 53:10-11).

In sin, man traded places with God. On the cross, Jesus returned the favor.

He took all the brokenness, all the fallenness, all the war and poverty and disease. He took the unspeakable acts of horror committed against the innocent and the unspoken acts of violence committed by the guilty. He took every foul thought, impure motive, and unholy imagining that you and I have experienced. He took every part of every brokenness, upon himself. He became detestable. He, the beautiful Son of God, became the most disgusting of things – sinfulness. He became all of this and, representing the sin of his people, he died. He killed sin. He destroyed death. The death of death was accomplished in the death of God the Son.

This is the kind of God he is. And, the great news about this self-sacrificing love is that anyone who would look upon the death of Jesus and believe that he died to save them, will be saved.[96] God is not only our judge, concerned with our righteousness; he is also the father of all those who would believe. He has the hairs on our head numbered[97] and all our days ordained beforehand.[98] He knows us better than anyone else and loves us more than we can possibly imagine.

> *In this is love, not that we have loved God but that he loved us and sent his Son to be the propitiation for our sins,* (1 John 4:10).

You can't know how much someone loves you until you know how much their love cost them. To love my wife in the covenant of marriage, I have happily relinquished my say over the rest of my life. I have joyfully given up independence, the love of other women, mobility, and a host of other things to gain her as my wife. And, that was a joy for me to do. Similarly, God's love for his people is the kind of love that willingly gives up the life of the Son of God to gain us – you and me – his people.

If God simply loved us with a less costly, more general kind of love, I suppose that would be nice. I can imagine even singing a song or two about it, but it's not transformational. To change the hard, stony heart into one that lives and beats for God requires more. That kind of love can only come from the demonstration of great sacrifice, and in this case the greatest sacrifice possible – the sacrifice of God himself.

This brings us to the third accomplishment of the death of Jesus Christ: reconciliation. In Ephesians, Paul tells us that sin separates us from God, creating an enormous chasm between us. He says:

> *Remember that you were at that time separated from Christ, alienated from [God's people] and strangers to the covenants of promise, having no hope and without God in the world. But now in Christ Jesus you who once were far off have been brought near by the blood of Christ,* (Ephesians 2:12-13).

---

[96] John 3:16

[97] *Even the hairs of your head are all numbered* (Matt. 10:30)

[98] *Your eyes saw my unformed substance; in your book were written, every one of them, the days that were formed for me when as yet there was none of them.* (Psalm 139:16)

Chapter Five – Redemption

God does not sit in Heaven shouting at us, "Come over here!" We can't. God, being unimaginably merciful to us, says, "I'm coming there." In coming and dying, he closes the gap and reconciles the world to himself.[99]

Remember that the nature of our offense against God spoiled creation in at least four distinct ways. Our first and primary problem is our separation from God. But in the cross of Christ, God was reconciling the world to himself, and then calling us to be partners with him, heralding and demonstrating that same reconciliation that we have received. Paul tells us, "all this is from God, who through Christ reconciled us to himself and gave us the ministry of reconciliation," (2 Cor. 5:18).

God has willingly sacrificed his son for a humanity that didn't deserve it, then how can we, the recipients of such a sacrifice, not extend the same reconciling grace to others?

> **What three things does Jesus' death accomplish for us, according to this section?**
> _____
> _____
> _____

THE RESURRECTION OF JESUS

Jesus not only died to destroy sin, but he rose to defeat its effects. In fact, didn't really rise from death, then all of Christianity is a sham, and its history inexplicable.[100] The entire Christian faith rises and falls upon the risen or fallen Jesus. If Jesus is alive, then the Scriptures are true, our faith is real, and our hope is sure. If Jesus is fallen, then so too falls Christianity. The good news is that there are a great number of reasons to understand that this event did happen.[101]

Thus, we have great hope.

Because Jesus was sinless, death (the effect of sin) had no hold on him. In rising from death, Jesus makes a mockery of death itself. In the ancient world, after one civilization conquered another, the conquered king and his family would be marched as captives back into the capital city of the conquering power. This was a humiliating prospect for any king, and this is precisely the kind of humiliation that death and the father of death received. Because he conquered death, all of death's companions

---

[99] 2 Corinthians 5:19

[100] The Apostle Paul left us no room for doubt here. He said that if Jesus is not actually alive, and we have no hope for a resurrection, then we are to be pitied above all people (2 Corinthians 15:21).

[101] For a fuller discussion of the historicity of the resurrection of Jesus, I recommend N.T. Wright, *The Resurrection of the Son of God*. (New York, NY: Fortress Press, 2003.) The book is a magisterial account on the historicity of the resurrection. For an introduction to the historicity of the resurrection, see *The Case for the Resurrection*, by Lee Strobel.

such as Satan, his fallen angels, and even disease and sickness are brought into open shame and humiliation. In short, the resurrection means victory – victory over sin, death, shame, guilt, and every other vile effect of sin. That is great news!

But still, Jesus' resurrection means something more. Death is not only conquered, but in the resurrection, Jesus secured a victory that is so powerful and far-reaching that death actually will be, in the end, swallowed up in the victory itself. Paul writes:

> *Death is swallowed up in victory... The sting of death is sin, and the power of sin is the law. But thanks be to God, who gives us the victory through our Lord Jesus Christ,* (1 Corinthians 15:54-57)

Jesus' victory over sin and death means that in him we too will find victory over sin and death. Jesus is a new kind of Adam.[102] He's the new head of the human race. Where Adam, our first father, led us into death, Jesus leads us into life and victory over death.

In a world full of the effects of sin and rebellion against God – disease, hurt, pain, war, poverty, hunger, abuse, and a host of other ills. In that kind of world, there is now hope. The resurrection of Jesus Christ from death means that in him we will find a victory – victory of such a kind that all of that will literally consume every last vestige of brokenness. This is the kind of future that God promises for those who identify with his life, death, and resurrection by grace through faith. But, such a victory is surely coming, because he himself promises, "He who raised the Lord Jesus will raise us also with Jesus and bring us with you into his presence." (2 Cor. 4:14)

In the doctrine of the resurrection we find all the hope in the world for the future. If God has raised Jesus from the dead, then it means that death is coming untrue. The plague released upon the universe because of man's disobedience is being turned upside down because of God's relentless love for man. The story of redemption finds its apex, and it's more surprising and wonderful than anything we would ever dream. God has won a decisive victory over our enemy. Victory is won, and the victory belongs to Jesus.

Read 1 Corinthians 15:1-4. What did Paul consider of first importance? Why is this summary important to you?

___

[102] In Romans 5:12-21, Paul unpacks the concept here. His basic argument is that Adam was a type, a foreshadowing of a better leader of the human race – Jesus Christ. In Christ, all can be forgiven and find victory over sin, just as Adam fell. "Therefore, as one trespass led to condemnation for all men, so one act of righteousness leads to justification and life for all men. For as by the one man's disobedience the many were made sinners, so by the one man's obedience the many will be made righteous," (Romans 5:18-19).

Chapter Five – Redemption

A NEW COVENANT PEOPLE

The final covenant has been made between God and humanity – the covenant of grace. God has given the terms: if we will identify with the life, death, and resurrection of Jesus then we will find our story in his. His great project of redemption is underway. The only question that remains is whether we wish to find ourselves within it or not. It's not a club one joins, there are no membership lists to check off, no character requirements. In this new covenant, God has given us something that we don't deserve. As the very thieves of his glory, why do we deserve a story of redemption? Why would God not just go ahead and judge everyone? The answer: grace.

Grace is God's unmerited favor. It cannot be earned. It is not deserved. It cannot be won, and it cannot be worked for. It is a free gift from God to us, and as such, it can only be received.

> *For by grace you have been saved through faith. And this is not your own doing; it is the gift of God, not a result of works, so that no one may boast,* (Ephesians 2:8-9).

All the stories, all the heroes of old, all the prophets – all of it was leading up to this moment – our moment in the story. You see, Jesus is like Noah's ark, but better. He bore us across the waters of God's judgment into a new life, even when we, much like Noah, didn't deserve it. Jesus is like Abraham, but better still. He obeyed God and left his heavenly home to go to the foreign land of earth to be the spiritual father of new sons and daughters who would bless the entire world. He is the one through whom all blessing would come in the promise given to Abraham. He's like the Day of Atonement, but perfect. He is our perfect sacrificial lamb, whose blood cleanses us from sin eternally, and who, like the second lamb, takes our sins away from us perfectly, leaving us spotless and whole before God.

All of it, the whole story ... it's all about him.

The question is, do you find yourself in the story? Do you look to Jesus as your ark, your leader, your sacrifice? And if you would like to, how do you do that? How can this story of redemption count for you?

QUESTIONS TO CONSIDER

1. Read Ephesians 2:1-4 and Romans 3:9-18. Is it possible for us to redeem ourselves? Why?

2. What is a covenant? How is the covenant love of God different than the way we normally experience love?

3. After the Fall, what did God do to cover Adam and Eve (Gen. 3)? Why did this happen?

4. Why did God save Noah? What was the result of Noah's faith?

5. Describe the pattern of redemption laid out on the chart in this chapter. How is this different from what you may have thought?

6. Who is Jesus, according to John 1:1-16?

Chapter Five – Redemption

7. According to C.S. Lewis' quote (pg. 118), why can't we just say that Jesus was a good teacher?

8. Describe Jesus' teaching ministry according to Mark 1:22.

9. Read Hebrews 9:26, 2 Corinthians 5:21, and Ephesians 2. Why did Jesus have to die? What did his death accomplish?

10. According to 1 John 4:9-10, how does the cross show us God's love?

11. Why is the resurrection of Jesus Christ important? What did it accomplish according to 1 Corinthians 15:55-56?

SCRIPTURE

Genesis 1-6

Ephesians 2:1-12

Isaiah 53:3-6

Genesis 12- 18

Romans 3:23-26

1 Corinthians 15

John 1:1-18

2 Corinthians 5:21

John 3:16

CHAPTER SIX

RESCUE

Chapter Six – Rescue

> *It's like everyone tells a story about themselves inside their own head. Always. All the time. That story makes you what you are. We build ourselves out of that story.*[103]

The stories we tell about ourselves are really important. The gospel story invites us to believe it – past mere imagination, into transformation. Ivan Illich, Austrian philosopher, priest, and social critic, notes the power of story in our lives, saying,

> *Neither revolution nor reformation can ultimately change society, rather you must tell a new powerful tale, one so persuasive that it sweeps away the old myths and becomes the preferred story, one so inclusive that it gathers all the bits of our past and our present into a coherent whole, one that even shines some light into our future so that we can take the next step. If you want to change society, then you have to tell an alternative story.*[104]

Like the society in which we live, we are shaped by those stories with which we identify. It turns out that somehow this story – this gospel – is the very power of God for the salvation, or rescue, of all who would believe it.[105] If we want to really be saved – rescued from sin and death – then this is the story we must embrace, believe, and trust.

Why is the story you believe about yourself and the world so important?
_____
_____
_____

RESCUED FROM WHAT?

God authored this grand narrative from Eden to Golgotha for a reason: to rescue us. But, this offer of salvation is meaningless to us unless we see that we need it. We must believe we need to be saved. You might imagine that our common brokenness would provide ample evidence for our need. War, famine, plague, death – evil is all around us. You'd think we'd be searching everywhere for our salvation. And, in a way we are. We go to school, we give our money, we pay our taxes, we give to charity, we move to Africa, we buy Fair Trade, and even eat organic – all in the hope that in some small way we're making the world

---

[103] Patrick Rothfuss, *The Name of the Wind*.

[104] Ivan Illich, quoted in Michael Frost and Alan Hirsch, *The Shaping of Things to Come*. (Baker: Grand Rapids, MI) 2003.

[105] Romans 1:16

better. But, are we? Or, are we simply masters at numbing our deep longing for salvation with little novocain shots of "good" work?

We've been deceived into believing that we can and should be the masters of our own destinies. It should come as no surprise, then, that a race of deceived people find little trouble deceiving themselves into thinking that they need no rescue, because there is no problem. Let's say it all together, "I'm okay. You're okay. Okay?"

But of course, we're *not* okay. To make sense of the salvation that Jesus has come to offer, we must be honest about our problem. Isaiah puts it like this:

> *Behold, the Lord's hand is not shortened, that it cannot save, or his ear dull, that it cannot hear; but your iniquities have made a separation between you and your God, and your sins have hidden his face from you so that he does not hear. (Isaiah 59:1-2).*

In Adam, our first father, we have all become corrupted by sin. But in Christ, we are offered a rescue from that corruption.

> *Your first father sinned, and your mediators transgressed against me. (Isaiah 43:27).*

> *Therefore, just as sin came into the world through one man, and death through sin, and so death spread to all men because all sinned.... But the free gift is not like the trespass. For if many died through one man's trespass, much more have the grace of God and the free gift by the grace of that one man Jesus Christ abounded for many. And the free gift is not like the result of that one man's sin. For the judgment following one trespass brought condemnation, but the free gift following many trespasses brought justification. (Romans 5:12, 15-16).*

Salvation is simply and magnificently the rescue which God, in his love for sinners like you and me, delivers us from his determined opposition to everything that would destroy us – judgement for sin. It's the wonderful result of the story of the gospel, that if believed by faith we might ourselves be rescued from God's determination to destroy sin, without us being destroyed along with it.

Re-read the Scriptures in this section. What are the effects of our sin? How does Jesus offer us rescue from sin?

_____
_____
_____

Chapter Six – Rescue

RESPONSE ONE: I DON'T NEED TO BE RESCUED

How do you respond this idea?

One response is offense. "I'm offended that you or anyone else would think that I'm 'lost,' or in need of some kind of rescue. I'm just fine." In the face of mounting evidence to the contrary, the only way you or I can maintain the claim, "I'm fine," is through self-deception – actually, a particular kind of self-deception called pride. Pride is that unique form of self-deception where we consider ourselves greater than we actually are. Now let me be careful here, as I'm not trying to offend you. Western pop-psychology tells us that pride is actually good. It's good to have self-esteem, it's important that you're confident.

Or perhaps in many ways, you are just fine. Maybe as your read this book your bank account is full, your car is fast, your health is sound, your job is secure, and all the planets in the solar system of you are spinning around quite nicely. It is precisely here that pride – that quiet, ultimate confidence in you and your own ability to control the world around you – lives. Inherent in material prosperity is the danger of proud self-sufficiency. In the West we know this well. Compared to other parts of the world, we don't lack for much. Most of us have jobs, food, healthcare, and a little bit of cash to get our favorite drink from our local overpriced coffee shop of choice. We're doing fine, and that is deadly to our perception of reality. Jesus spoke directly to this when he explained how difficult it is for the rich, powerful, and secure to inherit the Kingdom of God.[106] Those who have everything they want are almost universally unaware of the grace they so desperately need.

> *Again I tell you, it is easier for a camel to go through the eye of a needle than for a rich person to enter the kingdom of God. (Mt 19:24).*

But if we pause to consider the Christian story, the line, "I'm fine," should ring a bell. It's the same feeling of autonomy that our first parents must've experienced just before they reached out and took the fruits of rebellion.[107] It is this internal sense of self-sufficiency and self-contentment apart from God that is so very deadly. What we say when we claim, "I don't need to be rescued," is, "I'm good enough." We are satisfied with who we are, where we are, and what we are. We've become so pleased with our "good life" that we're blissfully unaware of the fact that we've merely decorated our prison cell more to our liking. Losing all hope for rescue from the shackles of sin, we've sought an armistice with our fallenness. We've come to think that we can save ourselves from our own issues.

And that – that, right there – is the lie.

No matter how nice the cell may be, without Jesus we're still in prison. And what's worse, there's nothing we can do about it. As the perpetrators of our own self-destruction, how could we think for a moment that rescue lies within? It must – it can only – come from somewhere, or someone, else.

---

[106] See Matthew 19:23-26, Luke 18:24-26 - What Jesus meant here is not that personal wealth is itself evil. However, the security that it brings along with it in this life can deceive those with great wealth into believing that they are in no need of anything at all, least of all the redeeming work of Jesus. This must be at least part of the reason that Jesus lays such a challenge to the wealthy to give generously, to keep them relying on God for their own provision in this life, and in the one to come.

[107] Genesis 3:6

Is there anything that is keeping you from seeking rescue in Jesus?

_____
_____
_____

RESPONSE TWO: I NEED A RESCUER

Jesus told a story about two men who came to pray. The first man was a good, religious man – a church-goer, generous with money, big bible in his hands, he approaches the altar for prayer. The second man was a tax collector, known to be a violent, thieving lot, he skulked up to the altar as well. The religious man prayed, "God, thank you for making me different than him. Thank you for making me religious, generous, and holy." Listening to this prayer, the thief simply bowed low and began to cry. As his tears stained the altar, he simply prayed, "God, have mercy on me. I'm a sinner."[108]

Only one of them went away forgiven.

As my friend Dr. Rice Broocks likes to say, the gospel is the only thing that can tell you what's really wrong with you. And me. And us. This "good news" as it's called is good news because it contrasts so brilliantly with the bad news that sits there like the elephant in the room of our lives. The second response to the gospel is acknowledging the elephant. "God, have mercy on me. I'm a sinner."

King David wrote Psalm 51 in a moment of sorrow over his sin. Read Psalm 51 and reflect on it. How does it resonate with you? Have you ever spoken this way to God?

_____
_____
_____

---

[108] This is taken from Luke 18:9-14.

Chapter Six – Rescue

THE HOPE WE'VE BEEN WAITING FOR

The story of redemption is like a great symphony which rises with beautiful melodies (creation). But the melody is struck with harsh dissonance (fall). Finally, after great dramatic development, the music crescendoes with an almost unbearable yearning, until resolution finally comes (redemption). This is the moment when the music resolves and the melody is rescued from the dissonance. This is the hope we've been waiting for.

Jesus came – divinity assuming finitude, perfection putting on decay. Curiously, it was God-human who was the first truly whole human – bearing God's image. No sacrifice was needed to atone for his sins. He wasn't born under the curse of Adam – he was the Son of God. He assumed our nature and showed us what God is like, inaugurating a new Kingdom, the borders of which have never stopped expanding since the day of his arrival. He died a substitutionary, vicarious, horrible death – taking upon himself not the consequences of his rebellion, but of ours. He experienced the hell of separation from God when he cried out from the cross, "My God, why have you forsaken me?" [109] He died, not because of someone taking his life from him, but in giving his life for us.[110] Ultimately, it was neither your sin nor mine which held Christ upon the nails, it was his love for sinners – a death by love.

> *I am the good shepherd. The good shepherd lays down his life for the sheep … No one takes it from me, but I lay it down of my own accord. I have authority to lay it down, and I have authority to take it up again. This charge I have received from my Father."* (John 10:11, 18).

He loved his people too much to leave them lost in their trespasses and sin. So, the promise given to the deceiver himself on that infamous day of humanity's treason was fulfilled. The snake-crusher had come. Three days after his horrific murder, he woke up from death as if from rest. Death had no rights to him because the rebellion placed upon him was not his, but ours. He walked, he taught, he ate, and he commissioned his disciples – that ragtag group of broken, hurting, and confused misfits – to go across the entire world and to make more disciples of Jesus.[111] He gave them the Holy Spirit as their power, comforter, and teacher. He commissioned them and empowered them to do all this and more, remembering the promise that if we are in him, we never lose him, and he never loses us.

Only Jesus has done what it takes to bring us to God. He alone offered a sacrifice great enough to cover all human guilt. He alone was worthy enough to come and redeem a world that had turned its back on God, turned inward toward self, and turned the world God loved toward Hell.

> *I am the way, and the truth, and the life. No one comes to the Father except through me.* (John 14:6).

> *The saying is trustworthy and deserving of full acceptance, that Christ Jesus came into the world to save sinners.* (1 Timothy 1:15).

---

[109] Mark 15:34, Matthew 27:46

[110] John 10:18

[111] Matthew 28:18-20

And there is salvation in no one else, for there is no other name under heaven given among men by which we must be saved." (Acts 4:12).

Salvation is the gift that God has bought for his people at the great cost of the life of his own son – one which he gives to us by grace. Like a great priest, Son of God perfectly represents God to us. As the Son of Man, he perfectly represents us to God. There is no other mediator between God and humanity, because there is no one else who could possibly do the job.

Why did Jesus do what he did? How does that affect you? What should your response be?
___
___
___

HOW ARE WE SAVED?

Something amazing happens when the better and truer story of the gospel supplants one we've been believing. But this exactly what *must* happen. *Your* story must end, and you must believe in the bigger story – the story of the gospel of Jesus Christ.

When you stop writing your own story and find yourself trusting in the gospel story for your salvation, you undergo a new birth – a conversion. If your life is to be changed by right doctrine, then this first and most vital connection must be made.

Amazingly, even this part involves God's grace. Our initial desire to even explore him is preceded and superseded by his desire to find us. This is what Paul meant when he said:

You were dead in the trespasses and sins in which you once walked ... But God, being rich in mercy, because of the great love with which he loved us, even when we were dead in our trespasses, made us alive together with Christ – by grace you have been saved... For by grace you have been saved through faith. And this is not your own doing; it is the gift of God, not a result of works, so that no one may boast. (Ephesians 2:1-2, 4-5, 8-9)

Dead people don't seek God. "But God..." *That* is one of the most beautiful phrases in the whole Bible. In this wonderful phrase we see that the truest and best of all theology can be summed up with three simple words: God saves us.

Chapter Six – Rescue

> **According to Ephesians 2:1-10, can we save ourselves? What is required?**
>
> _____
> _____
> _____

CONVERSION IS A GIFT

Left to our own devices, we're not coming to God. Remember, the Scriptures just said we were dead in our sins, not sick. Dead people don't do much, except perhaps feed worms. In any case, spiritually dead people certainly don't, on their own, go seeking out life in God.

> *None is righteous, no, not one; no one understands; no one seeks for God. All have turned aside; together they have become worthless; no one does good, not even one. Their throat is an open grave; they use their tongues to deceive. The venom of vipers is under their lips. Their mouth is full of curses and bitterness. Their feet are swift to shed blood; in their paths are ruin and misery, and the way of peace they have not known. There is no fear of God before their eyes.* (Romans 3:10b-18)

So how does it work? How is it possible that we, the spiritually dead, can take any advantage of what Jesus has done for us? The simple answer is that conversion starts with God. John Piper is helpful here when he says:

> *The native hardness of our hearts makes us unwilling and unable to turn from sin and trust the Savior. Therefore conversion involves a miracle of new birth. Thus new birth precedes and enables faith and repentance. Nevertheless, faith and repentance are our acts. We are accountable to do them. By the miracle of new birth, by pure grace, God grants us the inclination we need.*[112]

God calls us, and by grace we respond. Can we save ourselves? Of course not. This particular idea resonates with my own conversion to Christianity.

I remember being invited to a camp by one of my buddies when I was 11. At the time, I was so excited to break up the monotony of summer that I jumped at the opportunity. I didn't know what I was signing up for when I said yes, I just wanted to go to camp! As it turns out, it was a Christian camp. I vividly remember the message that changed my life. The camp pastor spoke from Revelation 3:20, where Jesus says:

> *Behold, I stand at the door and knock. If anyone hears my voice and opens the door, I will come in to him and eat with him, and he with me.*

---

[112] John Piper, *Desiring God*. Colorado Springs, CO: Multnomah. 1986, 62.

For the very first time I became aware – deeply aware – of the invitation of God to open the door of my life to his Son, Jesus. There were no charged emotions. It was as simple as me, a preteen boy, hearing the beautiful beckoning of God. At that moment all I wished to do was to be with him. There was no deep search. There was no good decision on my part to go look for him. He called, I came. I uttered a simple prayer, asking him to save me, and he did.

> **Read John 6:44. Can we come to God on our own terms? What is required first?**
> _____
> _____
> _____

REPENTING AND BELIEVING

Just like a newborn breathes in a big gasp of air and exhales a cry, when God saves us, we breathe in a deep chestful of grace and exhale thankful faith. The Scriptures echo this when they say:

> *If you confess with your mouth that Jesus is Lord and believe in your heart that God raised him from the dead, you will be saved,* (Romans 10:9).

Confession simply means to "say with." So, we're saying with all believers across all time, "Jesus, you are my risen Lord!" This is our confession. But to make this confession, we're also saying that everything else that formerly defined us and ruled us no longer does. So, confessing, "Jesus is Lord," is two-sided. These two sides are called repentance and faith.

Repentance and faith are deeply connected. Repenting involves turning around – changing one's mind. Repentance isn't just feeling bad about something. Plenty of people feel bad and don't change. That's not repentance, it's momentary sorrow. They aren't the same. Repentance leads to change. You know you've repented if you've changed. If repentance is the "turning from," then faith is the "turning to."

> *For godly grief produces a repentance that leads to salvation without regret, whereas worldly grief produces death.* (2 Corinthians 7:10).

If God has done all that he has said, then hasn't he earned our trust? If so, then turning from sin and trusting in Jesus for salvation is hardly a blind leap. It's placing one's hope for redemption in the fact of history that a man lived, died, and rose again from death, proving his divinity. That man is Jesus, and if those facts are true, then that man is worthy of trust (faith).

Chapter Six – Rescue

True faith involves at least three parts: knowledge, agreement, and reliance.[113]

First, knowledge. You can't believe in a thing that you don't know, just as you can't trust someone you've never met. Paul says, "how are they to hear without someone preaching, and how are they to preach unless they are sent?" (Rom. 10:14-15) He's asking a rhetorical question to motivate his audience (in this case, the church in Corinth) to the mission of telling the Gospel story.

Second, we must agree that the story we know is true. You know the story of Goldilocks and the Three Bears, but none of us really believe there was a little girl who wandered into the remote forest home of a bear family. The gospel, of course, is different. Because this is a story that took place in real history, we must come to not merely be aware of it, but to believe that it actually happened – that it is true. A merely symbolic, Jesus-is-risen-in-my-heart kind of fairytale won't do. When the story of a God who has come to die that you might live forever with him melts your heart, you don't agree with it, you believe it.

Finally, you must rely on that story for yourself. It's here that the real gap between life and doctrine exists. As a pastor, I often wonder how many in my own church and churches where I've served have knowledge of the gospel, and even agree with it, but don't have this final, critical piece – reliance. We can't just know right facts and agree, we must trust fully in the central character of the story, Jesus Christ. True, biblical faith cannot remain merely in the category of mental ascent. If that describes you at the moment, then I implore you to heed the words of James, the brother of Jesus:

> ...faith by itself, if it does not have works, is dead. But someone will say, "You have faith and I have works." Show me your faith apart from your works, and I will show you my faith by my works. You believe that God is one; you do well. Even the demons believe – and shudder! (James 2:17-19).

Real faith must move beyond the realm of knowledge and agreement into reliance. Life must be connected to the doctrine of the gospel. So, when the gospel comes to us, we respond by turning from every pursuit that was taking us away from Christ and follow him, not by merely agreeing with where he is going, but by going there with him. We cease putting our trust in ourselves, in living for ourselves, and in satisfying ourselves, and we look to Jesus to be our rescuer, our savior, our treasure, and our master.

> Seek the LORD while he may be found; call upon him while he is near; let the wicked forsake his way, and the unrighteous man his thoughts; let him return to the LORD, that he may have compassion on him, and to our God, for he will abundantly pardon. (Isaiah 55:6-7).

Have you repented and believed the gospel? If not, why not?

___

[113] I have taken this observation from Dr. Wayne Grudem in his lectures and works on systematic theology. He states these three ideas as "knowledge, approval, and trust." I've modified them slightly for my purposes here, but owe the original thought to him.

Rescue – **Chapter Six**

THE EXCHANGE

The moment we trust Jesus a wonderful transaction takes place. We are justified – made right and righteous before God. The moment before our faith in Christ, and every moment leading up to it, we were dead in our sins – unable to see God, love God, serve God, know God, or decide to follow God.[114] But the moment we repent and believe the gospel, everything changes.

Justification is complex to theologians. Countless books have been written to drill down into the exact nature of this doctrine. But what is complicated to the theologian is simple to the man or woman who has experienced it. This glorious exchange means that, because of Christ's perfect obedience, substitutionary death, and victorious resurrection, God views us differently. It is an instantaneous change of our status before God where he considers our sins as forgiven in Christ and views Christ's righteousness, all his good works and obedience, as our very own.

Martin Luther knew a thing or two about what it meant to be made right with God. The question, "How can I, a sinner, stand before God and be accepted?" burned within his soul as a young monk. So perturbed was he by this question that, when he finally discovered the answer, it sparked a revolution that we now call the Reformation. During that time, he penned these immortal words about justification:

> *This is that mystery which is rich in divine grace to sinners: wherein by a wonderful exchange our sins are no longer ours but Christ's, and the righteousness of Christ not Christ's but ours. He has emptied himself of his righteousness that he might clothe us with it and fill us with it; and he has taken our evils upon himself that he might deliver us from them.*[115]

Our sins for his sinlessness. Our rebellion for his obedience. Our shame for his glory.

He traded his life for the death we deserved, so that in him we might find life that we don't deserve, by grace. This is rescue. This is salvation. This is what Paul meant when he said,

> *For our sake he made him to be sin who knew no sin, so that in him we might become the righteousness of God,* (2 Corinthians 5:21).

According to this section, what happens when we repent and believe the gospel?
_____
_____
_____

---

[114] See Romans 3:9-18, Ephesians 2:1-3

[115] Martin Luther, *Werke* (Weimar, 1883)

Chapter Six – Rescue

ALL OF GRACE

The fact cannot be stated enough that we do nothing to earn a right standing before God. We sin because we're sinful. We act broken because we are, in fact, broken. How ridiculous, then, is the idea that we – the broken, breakers of ourselves and others – can fix ourselves? This is the lie of religion. "You're broken," says religion, "so do these things to fix yourself. Go to church, stop sinning, and try harder." This is not the gospel, because it is not good news.

God has much better news for us than giving us a self-improvement check-list. God doesn't help those who help themselves. God doesn't meet us halfway as long as we seek him hard enough. God reaches down out of heaven and rescues us – helpless, weak, and dead in sin. Applying the grace of Jesus Christ, by the power of the Spirit, he saves us entirely by his free, precious grace.

> *For all have sinned and fall short of the glory of God, and are justified by his grace as a gift.* (Romans 3:23-24).

> *For by grace you have been saved through faith. And this is not your own doing; it is the gift of God, not a result of works, so that no one may boast.* (Ephesians 2:8-9).

> *Let us then with confidence draw near to the throne of grace, that we may receive mercy and find grace to help in time of need.* (Hebrews 4:16).

Spurgeon reminds us of the lavishness of God's grace in Jesus when he writes:

> *Our Lord Jesus is ever giving, and does not for a solitary instant withdraw his hand. As long as there is a vessel of grace not yet full to the brim, the oil shall not be stayed. He is a sun ever-shining; he is manna always falling round the camp; he is a rock in the desert, ever sending out streams of life from his smitten side; the rain of his grace is always dropping; the river of his bounty is ever-flowing, and the well-spring of his love is constantly overflowing.*[116]

What does it mean to say that we are 'saved by grace?'
_____
_____
_____

---

[116] Charles Haddon Spurgeon, *Morning and Evening*.

CLEAN

Like the spotless animal slain by the priests for sin, Jesus was slain for all the sins of his people. The death of Jesus grants us an additional benefit – a doctrine called *expiation*. As we are justified and given the righteousness of Christ (2 Cor. 5:21, Rom. 4:3, 6), we are also set free from the stain of sin itself. Expiation is the glorious truth that Jesus died to make us clean – clean of sins committed by us, and those committed *against* us.

This is a beautiful truth, especially for victims, the oppressed, and the poor. Jesus isn't simply the one who forgives the sins *you've* committed. He also removes all the sins that have been committed against you.

According to a study done by the U.S. Department of Justice, nearly one-third of American women report being sexually abused or mistreated at some point in their lives.[117] How amazing to know that if you've been victimized and felt dirty, ugly, and worthless, then the cross of Christ has glorious, purifying news for you. In Christ you can be clean – truly and totally clean.

> *...as far as the east is from the west, so far does he remove our transgressions from us* (Psalm 103:12).

After having established himself as a successful businessman in Chicago near the end of the 19th century, things began to slowly unravel in Horatio Spafford's life. He lost a four-year-old son to scarlet fever. A year after that, the great fire of Chicago destroyed many of his real estate investments. Two years later, the Spafford family decided to vacation in England. Horatio was detained on business but decided to send his wife and four daughters ahead of him. On November 22, 1873, their vessel was struck by another, and there in the cold waters of the North Atlantic, Spafford's four daughters lost their lives. His wife, Anna, was the lone survivor, and upon arriving in England sent a telegram back to her husband which read simply, "saved alone." Spafford boarded the next vessel for England, and crossing the same seas that stole away his beloved daughters, he penned this verse of his famous hymn:

> *My sin, oh the bliss of this glorious thought, my sin, not in part, but the whole, was nailed to the cross and I bear it no more, Praise the Lord! Praise the Lord, oh my soul!*

Something about the glorious gospel story freed Spafford from both the evils he had committed, but most vividly, the evils that befell him. His life was saved because of the beauty of the doctrine of justification and the doctrine of expiation.

What does the doctrine of expiation mean? What does it mean for you?
_____
_____
_____

---

[117] Taken from the Commonwealth Fund Survey, 1998. Cited from *National Domestic Violence Statistics*. <http://www.domesticpeace.com/ed_nationalstats.html>

Chapter Six – Rescue

A CHANGED LIFE, CHANGING

At the moment of your conversion, you really are changed. But, you're not done changing. That is, you're not perfect. Not yet, anyway. If justification is an instantaneous legal change from unrighteous to righteous, then sanctification is the day-by-day becoming – the process of growing to be more and more like Jesus. After our hearts are changed instantly before God, our lives follow suit day-by-day. The Apostle Paul pleaded with his Roman fellow believers in this way:

> *I appeal to you therefore, brothers, by the mercies of God, to present your bodies as a living sacrifice, holy and acceptable to God, which is your spiritual worship. Do not be conformed to this world, but be transformed by the renewal of your mind. (Romans 12:1-2)*

And to the Philippian Christians,

> *Brothers, I do not consider that I have made it my own. But one thing I do: forgetting what lies behind and straining forward to what lies ahead, I press on toward the goal for the prize of the upward call of God in Christ Jesus. (Philippians 3:13-14)*

After we repent from everything that takes us away from God, and by grace through faith obtain the rescue that God offers, a new life begins. It becomes the joyful journey of the disciple to grow more like the savior. It's a journey that is empowered by God's grace, and striven for by our hardest work. It's God who is at work within us to change our minds and empower our efforts to become more like him.

The journey of sanctification fuses man's responsibility, God's work, and the Church's discipleship in the process of the new life of the follower of Jesus. In this process, God begins to reform and renew all kinds of things in our lives, including:

- Thoughts

    Do not be conformed to this world, but be transformed by the renewal of your mind. (Ro 12:2).

    Put off your old self, which belongs to your former manner of life and is corrupt through deceitful desires, and to be renewed in the spirit of your minds, and to put on the new self (Ephesians 4:22-24).

- Habits

    Let not sin therefore reign in your mortal body, to make you obey its passions. Do not present your members to sin as instruments for unrighteousness, but present yourselves to God as those who have been brought from death to life, and your members to God as instruments for righteousness. (Romans 6:12-13).

- Sexuality

    For this is the will of God, your sanctification: that you abstain from sexual immorality; that each one of you know how to control his own body in holiness and honor (1 Thessalonians 4:3-4).

- Language

   Let no corrupting talk come out of your mouths, but only such as is good for building up, as fits the occasion, that it may give grace to those who hear… (Ephesians 4:29).

- Money

   You will be enriched in every way to be generous in every way, which through us will produce thanksgiving to God. (2 Corinthians 9:11).

Notice what is being said. God doesn't demand we change so he can accept us. God accepts us by the grace of the gospel and begins to change us. All of us have a journey from the starting point of our faith to the final day with God. But we can be confident and trusting, because…

He who began a good work in you will bring it to completion at the day of Jesus Christ. (Philippians 1:6).

> **You just read, "God doesn't demand we change so he can accept us. God accepts us by the grace of the gospel and begins to change us." Are you ready and willing to allow God to change you?**
> _____
> _____
> _____

WHY CAN'T GOD JUST FORGIVE US?

Real forgiveness, is very costly.

As a pastor, I'm often asked, "Why can't God just forgive us? Why a cross? Why blood?" These questions have good philosophical and theological answers, and we'll come to those. But, these questions often come from the heart, not just the head. The idea that someone had to suffer a bloody, terrible death for us is tough to accept – worse still the sad torment of separation from God which awaits those who refuse such grace.

To help shed some light on this question, let's look at four ideas: (1) Real forgiveness is very costly, (2) if God didn't act justly toward sin, then he wouldn't be good or just, (3) God's love means that God must be just, or he wouldn't be loving, and (4) Hell exists, and is the eternal consequence of our temporal desires.

Chapter Six – Rescue

First, real forgiveness is very costly. Let me give an example. I remember being home from the mission field as a younger man, borrowing my father's new car. On one occasion, I had my 4-year-old daughter with me and we were driving to a friend's home. We arrived, the friend came outside, and we began talking, when, unknown to me, my daughter had innocently found a pen and began to draw a picture … on the leather upholstery. Embarrassed, I called my dad and offered to pay for the damage. Graciously, he replied, "You're a missionary, Adam, and you people aren't known for having extra money. I'll take care of it."

Notice in this story that there was real damage to my father's car. It wasn't imaginary. Someone was going to have to pay for it, me or him, or perhaps we share it, but someone had pay to fix what was broken. In this instance, forgiveness meant bearing the cost of a new armrest. So, God is left with a dilemma. Shall he make us pay for the sin debt, or shall he bear the cost? The glorious news of the Gospel is that God chose to bear the cost entirely because humanity was unable to pay the bill. In his body, Christ purchased the cost for a new, perfect, sinless, shalom-laden universe where God dwells with his people forever. Forgiveness is costly indeed, and the good news is that God has paid the debt.

Second, we must see that if God didn't act justly toward sin, then he wouldn't be good or just. Imagine that someone raped and murdered a member of your family. The police catch him and his trial begins. Evidence is presented, the jury is convinced, and the verdict is delivered: guilty. However, at the last minute, the judge pipes up and says, "I understand that you are guilty and you deserve to be punished. However, I'm a loving, kind judge. I can't imagine a fellow member of the human race having to suffer in jail for the rest of their lives. So, I'm commuting your sentence. You're free to go, just don't do it again."

Is that a good judge? Certainly not. And yet, we often feel as though God is not just to judge us according to our actions. No one has a problem thinking that God should judge "those people." But as for us and the people we like, we can scarcely imagine it. That's because we're hypocrites. We want justice to crush those who hurt us but overlook us when we hurt others.

Third, in order for God to be truly loving toward us, he must judge us. Love and wrath are entangled. In the previous illustration we saw that if God were to simply sweep sin under the rug, he'd be doing injustice to those who had suffered at the hands of the wrongdoer. But in fact, if God is going to show himself as loving, he must judge us and everyone else.

Imagine again that your sister is addicted to drugs. One day on your way to work you see her buying the drugs that are destroying her life from a man on the street corner. How do you feel toward that man, toward those drugs, even toward your sister? Hurt. Sadness. And what else? Wrath. When you see that loved one being ruined by someone or something, you become filled with wrath – a determined opposition to that which will destroy the one you love.

> *Think how we feel when we see someone we love ravaged by unwise actions or relationships. Do we respond with benign tolerance as we might toward strangers? Far from it … Anger isn't the opposite of love. Hate is, and the final form of hate is indifference … God's wrath is not a cranky explosion, but his settled opposition to the cancer … which is eating out the insides of the human race he loves with his whole being.*[118]

God has provided a way for humanity to be reconciled, for debt to be paid, for his never-stopping love to reform the hearts of men and women. But, this good news has a necessary and opposite down side: some people simply will not accept the story. What is to become of them? What is to become of those who don't trust in Jesus as Lord, savior, master, treasure, and friend? God is just, and is determined to destroy that which destroys us, even if we, in the end, identify more with our own brokenness and rebellion than we do with him. This terrible reality is called Hell.

---

[118] Rebecca Pippert, *Hope Has Its Reasons*. Harper, 1990, Chapter 4. Quoted from Tim Keller, *The Reason for God*. New York, NY: Dutton, 2008, 73.

Hell is extremely uncomfortable to think about. How many of us have seen those fear-inspiring Renaissance paintings of demons with pitchforks dragging poor, unwitting people down to the fiery torment which awaits them? Who wants to think about that? Who wants to imagine that someone they love, or even someone they're merely well-acquainted with, might spend eternity in such a setting? No one, of course. And yet, such a concept seems firmly lodged in the religious consciousness of most people. But, is it Scriptural?

Hell is certainly Scriptural. Jesus spoke more about Hell than anyone else.

> *There was a rich man who was clothed in purple and fine linen and who feasted sumptuously every day. And at his gate was laid a poor man named Lazarus, covered with sores, who desired to be fed with what fell from the rich man's table. Moreover, even the dogs came and licked his sores. The poor man died and was carried by the angels to Abraham's side. The rich man also died and was buried, and in Hades, being in torment, he lifted up his eyes and saw Abraham far off and Lazarus at his side. And he called out, 'Father Abraham, have mercy on me, and send Lazarus to dip the end of his finger in water and cool my tongue, for I am in anguish in this flame.' But Abraham said, 'Child, remember that you in your lifetime received your good things, and Lazarus in like manner bad things; but now he is comforted here, and you are in anguish. And besides all this, between us and you a great chasm has been fixed, in order that those who would pass from here to you may not be able, and none may cross from there to us.' And he said, 'Then I beg you, father, to send him to my father's house– for I have five brothers–so that he may warn them, lest they also come into this place of torment.' But Abraham said, 'They have Moses and the Prophets; let them hear them.' And he said, 'No, father Abraham, but if someone goes to them from the dead, they will repent.' He said to him, 'If they do not hear Moses and the Prophets, neither will they be convinced if someone should rise from the dead.'*
> (Luke 16:19-31)

Here there are two characters: a nameless rich man and a poor man named Lazarus. The rich man was someone who didn't look to God to justify his life and give him meaning and purpose. Instead he looked to earthly wealth. He was successful. The single most identifying characteristic of his life was his pursuit of money, so much so that he never even noticed the poor man laid at his gate. His treasure, his focus, even his name in the story, are all related to his wealth.

Actually, it's his name which gives us a clue to what Hell is really like. In the story, the rich man gets no name. He's just "the rich man." He simply becomes more and more of what he wanted most in life. His eternal destiny was the logical outcome of his temporal preferences. In Hell, he was still trying to boss Lazarus around: trying to get Lazarus to bring him water, and ordering Lazarus to go see his family. Even in the midst of torment, he thought he was better than the poor man. He thought because of his status as a wealthy man he ought to be served.[119] On into eternity, he became the consequence of his choice. Selfishness and greed became the fires which consumed him forever.

> *Life with God is big. Life without God is small. Life without God is hell. Hell is not a chamber God locks from the outside against our repentant will; it is a closet we latch from the inside through our unrepentant will.*[120]

---

[119] I am very grateful to Dr. Tim Keller's observations on this passage in his book *The Reason for God* and in his various sermons and lectures on the topic.

[120] Butler, Joshua Ryan. *The Skeletons in God's Closet: The Mercy of Hell, the Surprise of Judgment, the Hope of Holy War* (pp. 99-100). Thomas Nelson.

Chapter Six – Rescue

Sin, as we saw, is much more than merely the breaking of God's laws, it's the inversion of God's world. Instead of enjoying creation to worship God, we worship creation instead of God. Augustine was right when he called sin disordered love[121] – we love God's creation (money, sex, power, education, family, environment, etc.) more than we love God himself. If some created thing is the functional god of our entire earthly life, then God, in the end, gives us what we most desire ... us alone with our idolatry, away from him forever. This is one of the points of the parable that Jesus was telling. If we don't accept the rescue, if we don't find ourselves in the story of redemption, then we are simply left with our story, which is usually just a sad tale of us struggling to get what we most want out of life, what we most desire. And in the end, if we desire something other than God, then God gives us what we want. C.S. Lewis wrote,

> *There are only two kinds of people in the end: those who say to God, 'Thy will be done,' and those to whom God says, in the end, 'Thy will be done.'*[122]

So no, God cannot simply forgive at no cost to us or himself. Real forgiveness is costly. Because he is good and just, he cannot simply abolish the debt that humanity has incurred. Because he is loving, he is ultimately and decidedly opposed to sin, because it's killing the people he loves. The brokenness of sin must be dealt with, either by the gracious sacrifice of Christ on the cross, or by us, should we reject Christ's sacrifice. According to the Christian Scriptures, those are the options. Praise God that in love, he has given a redeemer.

What are the four reasons that God can't "just forgive us?" What questions about this do you still have?
_____
_____
_____

WHAT MUST I DO TO BE SAVED?

What must I do to be saved?

That was the question burning in the hearts of the men and women who heard Peter's impassioned proclamation on the day of Pentecost. The most horrible crime that humanity has ever committed had just occurred – the murder of the Son of God. But three days later, he rose again. Then he appeared to hundreds of people. This news – this magnificent story came to a dramatic moment of tension when Peter confronted the people of Jerusalem about all that had occurred. Filled with the Holy Spirit, Peter explained how everything that happened was part of God's plan to rescue his people, but that the blood of God's son was on their hands. Trembling, they asked the only question that made sense. "What must I do to be saved?" Peter responded,

---

[121] Augustine, *The City of God.* 15. 22

[122] C.S. Lewis, *The Great Divorce.* Chapter 9.

> *Repent and be baptized every one of you in the name of Jesus Christ for the forgiveness of your sins, and you will receive the gift of the Holy Spirit. For the promise is for you and for your children and for all who are far off, everyone whom the Lord our God calls to himself.*
> (Acts 2:38-39).

This is the greatest intersection between life and doctrine that must – absolutely must – occur. Perhaps as you're reading this, you find yourself identifying with God's great redemption story. God seems to be calling you to himself, so how should you respond?

You start by repenting – turning from what you now recognize is keeping you from God – sin. You must see it for what it is, see that you are walking with your back to God. Then, you must put your back to sin, asking Jesus to forgive you, and enable you to change.

> *Repent therefore, and turn back, that your sins may be blotted out, that times of refreshing may come from the presence of the Lord, and that he may send the Christ appointed for you, Jesus...* (Acts 3:19-20).

But don't only repent. Believe the gospel. Don't merely agree with its facts, but believe Jesus' words in such a way that it shows up in your life.

Once you've done that, pray. Ask God to change you, make you new, and accept you into his family. And then, rise from your knees to new life in Christ, bound together with the people of God. Turn from sin, trust the savior, and belong to the family of God's people.

Then, you shall be rescued.

Have you repented and believed the gospel? If not, why not?
___
___
___

Chapter Six – Rescue

QUESTIONS TO CONSIDER

1. Read Romans 1:16-18. How did Paul feel about the gospel? Do you believe this? Have you personally trusted in Jesus to save you from your sins?

   _____
   _____
   _____

2. After hearing the gospel, do you feel that you need to be rescued from sin? Why?

   _____
   _____
   _____

3. According to Acts 4:12, is there hope for salvation in anyone else other than Jesus? Why?

   _____
   _____
   _____

4. Read Revelation 3:20. Have you personally opened the door of your heart to Jesus? If not, are you willing to right now?

   _____
   _____
   _____

5. Do you believe that Jesus Christ is Lord and that God raised him from the dead? (Romans 10:9)

   _____
   _____
   _____

6. According to Acts 2:38-39, what must you do to be in right relationship with God?

   _____
   _____
   _____

7. What are the three parts of faith mentioned in this chapter?

8. Read Romans 3:23-24 and Ephesians 2:8-9. What is grace? Have you experienced God's grace?

9. After we repent and trust in Christ, what does Jesus do with our sin?

10. Have you trusted fully in Christ and received his rescue? If so, describe that experience. If not, are you willing to?

Chapter Six – Rescue

SCRIPTURE

Genesis 1-6
Ephesians 2:1-12
Isaiah 53:3-6

Genesis 12-18
Romans 3:23-26
1 Corinthians 15

John 1:1-18
2 Corinthians 5:21
John 3:16

SECTION THREE

CHANGE

CHAPTER SEVEN

BEING

Chapter Seven – Being

The term *Christian* was first ascribed to the followers of Jesus in the city of Antioch.[123] It was never meant to be the name of a religion. The term was first used to mock Jesus' disciples. But here we are, thousands of years later, happily wearing the word that means "little Christ." But what is a Christian, exactly? Are you Christian if you attend church? Avoid sin? Read the Bible?

Simply put, a Christian is a follower of Jesus Christ. Like the earliest followers, Christians are disciples – those people who have repented of sin and put all their trust in Jesus – people who do what he does, go where he goes, and say what he'd say. But what does that look like? What does it mean to be a follower of Jesus and become more like Christ as we follow him?

In Mark 1, the Gospel writer gives a short, direct description of Jesus' call to his disciples. We read:

> *Passing alongside the Sea of Galilee, he saw Simon and Andrew the brother of Simon casting a net into the sea, for they were fishermen. And Jesus said to them, "Follow me, and I will make you become fishers of men." And immediately they left their nets and followed him.* (Mark 1:16-18)

From this passage, we can note two features of being a disciple: a disciple follows Jesus, and a disciple fishes for men and women. Breaking these down further, I believe that following Jesus means that Jesus becomes for the disciple his greatest treasure and his life's trajectory. Fishing for men and women means that disciples have a new mission in life, and a new power to fulfill it.

Have you repented and believed the gospel? If not, why not?
_____
_____
_____

A NEW TREASURE

> *The kingdom of heaven is like treasure hidden in a field, which a man found and covered up. Then in his joy he goes and sells all that he has and buys that field.* (Matthew 13:44)

Earlier we read about Augustine's definition of sin: disordered love. This idea has its roots, of course. Augustine was a man plagued by lust when he came to faith in Christ. Today we might call him a sex addict. Sex was his treasure and delight. How did he change? Therapy? Positive self-confession? No. Fundamentally, Augustine experienced what we all must experience if we are to follow Jesus. What he thought was most valuable – his treasure – changed. Like Augustine's disordered love of sex,

---

[123] Acts 11:26

all our disordered loves start to be put in their proper place when we love Jesus more. And we do love him more, because he's more lovely than everything else.

Christians are to be like the man in the parable above. We have providentially happened upon the greatest treasure of all. So happily we sell everything – even very nice things – for the better thing. God alone satisfies the desire of our hearts. Sin imprisons us in a dungeon of lesser joys, lower loves, and a dingy, fading satisfaction. But when we repent and follow Jesus, all that changes. John Wesley's hymn says it well:

> *Long my imprisoned spirit lay, fast bound in sin and nature's night;*
> *Thine eye diffused a quickening ray – I woke, the dungeon flamed with light;*
> *My chains fell off, my heart was free, I rose, went forth, and followed Thee.*
> *My chains fell off, my heart was free, I rose, went forth, and followed Thee!*[124]

The hymn doesn't say, "I followed thee because I owed it to thee," or, "I followed thee so thou couldst give me earthly riches." What was the treasure that caused Wesley to leave the prison of self-satisfaction? What caused him to rise and follow? Jesus.

As I have taught people over the years to seek their greatest joy and delight in Jesus, I have noticed two general errors that often arise. The first we might call the error of austerity – thinking that we ought to merely obey God and do our duty, not seek our pleasure in him. It's the total rejection of any concern for pleasure in God. The second is just the opposite. Call it the error of prosperity – the fixation of our pleasure in God's things, instead of God himself. To test yourself, see how you complete this sentence: "I follow God so that I can _____."

Perhaps you answered something like, "Obey," or, "Do what I ought to do." This is the austerity error. To you, I would simply ask, what is your most natural response when something really amazing happens to you? Joy. If you're given a birthday gift, a bonus at work, or a visit from a friend whom you've not seen for years, you experience joy. And, in enjoying those blessings, you tell of their worth. If I surprised you with your favorite meal, you'd experience joy. But, imagine I flew a dear but distant friend to visit you. You'd experience much more joy from the friend than the meal. Why? Because the friend is better than the meal. In the same way, when the gospel brings us into relationship with Jesus, our joy should reach an even higher peak, because he is better.[125]

But maybe you're nothing like the austere man I'm talking to in the previous paragraph. Maybe you answer the question differently. Perhaps you'd say, "I follow God so that I can have a better life: a blessed family, a great career, and more money." This is the prosperity error, and it will do nothing but rob you of joy in Jesus. Imagine you're a parent out with your children at a store. They are acting up, and you're correcting them constantly. Then, when you walk by the toy aisle, all of a sudden they become dutifully obedient. "Yes ma'am" and "thank you" abounds, all with the hopes that you, their parent, will give them a toy for their efforts. We have a word for this kind of behavior – manipulation. In this example, the children aren't obeying out of a heart to love and please their parents, but out of a selfish desire to get their parents' stuff. If we're not careful, we can treat God the same way.

---

[124] Charles Wesley, *And Can it Be that I should Gain?* Hymn from *Psalms and Hymns*, 1738.

[125] Few books have changed my life in the way the Dr. John Pipers' book, Desiring God has. This phrase forms the thesis of that book: God is most glorified in us when we are most satisfied in him. This glorious truth has rescued me from a natural inclination of my heart to make following Jesus a game of check-the-box duty. I cannot recommend it to you highly enough.

Chapter Seven – Being

Trying to manipulate God with obedience so that he will bless you with more trinkets is not the reason the Savior spilled his blood. He was wounded so that we could get him. Follow Jesus to get Jesus.

> *For Christ also suffered once for sins, the righteous for the unrighteous, that he might bring us to God.*
> (1 Peter 3:18)

The goal of the Christian life is God. Jesus loved his Father more than anything else – even his own life. In fact, he was willing to give up his life just to share with us the incomparable joy of knowing the Father the way he does. This is why you were made – the fulfillment of your design.

The gospel simply returns us to our original design specifications. We were made for God. He is the fuel our souls were designed to burn.[126] The Westminster Catechism puts it like this:

> *Q: What is the chief end of man?*
>
> *A: The chief end of man is to glorify God and enjoy him forever.*

Christians are not people who've adopted new religious jobs to get God to like them. Christians have been adopted by a God who already loves them, so we obey. When God, by sheer mercy, adopts one of us as a son or daughter, we experience joy and God is glorified. Convinced of this fact, John Piper altered the above statement by changing a simple word:

> *The chief end of man is to glorify God BY enjoying him forever.*[127]

We do not glorify God through the heartless, unhappy performance of religious rituals. Behavior like that doesn't glorify anyone. You and I don't make God look great and glorious when we begrudgingly read our Bibles and show up late to church. But, when we are so excited about Jesus that we can barely contain it, then God gets glory, and we get joy.

This is how Augustine fought back the sin in his own heart, by crowding it out with joy in God. He writes in his *Confessions*:

> *You have made us for yourself, oh Lord, and our hearts are restless until they find their rest in you.*[128]

Enjoy God. Come and ask him for the ability to enjoy him more. There is no greater source of pleasure, because all other sources end. There is no deeper ocean of joy, because all other joys prove shallow. Let your heart learn to do what David's did, to long to meet with the God who has rescued you.

> *As a deer pants for flowing streams, so pants my soul for you, O God. My soul thirsts for God, for the living God. When shall I come and appear before God?* (Psalm 42:1-2).

---

[126] Lewis, *Mere Christianity*.

[127] John Piper, *Desiring God*.

[128] St. Augustine, *The Confessions of St. Augustine*. Book I.I.

> **How is enjoying God connected to glorifying God? Read Psalm 42:1-2. Is this your experience of God?**
> _____
> _____
> _____

A NEW TRAJECTORY

We will always pursue what is precious to us.

Once our hearts have been melted by the gospel, we cannot go on living the way we were. The trajectory of our lives changes from living for self to living for God. Notice the order here. Jesus doesn't demand our obedience and then become our delight. Instead his relentless love for us turns our hearts, we are converted, and obedience follows. Therefore, the Christian loves to follow God in obedience because he delights to call Christ his friend.[129]

Living this way involves a process called progressive sanctification. Progressive, because it happens over your whole life. Sanctification, because over your life you're growing in holiness and Christlikeness.

Following Jesus doesn't mean becoming a moralistic curmudgeon. It means doing what he does, loving what he loves, hating what he hates, and walking like he walks. As we do that, will we be convicted by word and Spirit to change? Certainly. We cannot run after two finish lines. Pursuing God means abandoning those things that keep us from him, and running toward the new finish line – Christ.

Consider these words from the author of Hebrews:

> *...let us also lay aside every weight, and sin which clings so closely, and let us run with endurance the race that is set before us, looking to Jesus, the founder and perfecter of our faith...* (Hebrews 12:1-2a)

Perhaps you're thinking, "That all sounds great, but how do I do that?" Anyone who has ever tried to change knows how hard it is. Just think of gym memberships after New Year's Day. We start with good intentions but almost always fail. If we can't lose five pounds how can we ever expect to live for Jesus? How do we do it? How do we "lay aside every weight and sin?" How can we even want to do that?

It's impossible.

---

[129] *You are my friends if you do what I command you.* (John 15:14).

Chapter Seven – Being

It's totally, completely impossible for you to stop doing wrong. It is, however, possible for you to want something else – or someone else – more.

Thomas Chalmers, a 19th century Scottish pastor is famous for his phrase, "the expulsive power of a new affection." The genius of his idea was his awareness that we can't just stop loving our sins and weights. But, you can replace sin with something better, if you encounter something, or someone, more satisfying. When Jesus is the master of your life, you follow him because he is better than the previous pursuit.

> ...work out your own salvation with fear and trembling. For it is God who works in you, both to will and to work for his good pleasure. (Philippians 2:12b-13)

What an incredible thought. We are commanded to work out the implications of our rescue, assured that all the while God is working within us to do it. You're not passive, sitting around waiting for God to wave his hand over your head to magically make you holy. Nor are you active – doing all the growing on your own, pulling yourself up by your bootstraps. Instead, you are cooperative. You work, he works. He wills, you will. Growth toward God is like the plant which grows toward the sunlight. The plant reaches its stem toward the Sun, the Sun beckons it upward.

Across the centuries, Christians have engaged in many disciplines. Reading and thinking on the Scriptures. Praying. Fasting. Worshipping. All of these and more are the actions of one whose heart is set on growing toward God.

You only have one throne in your life, and only one person can occupy it. If Christ is truly Lord, then self and selfish desires can no longer be. This means that followers of Jesus never, ever have a reason to give a final victory to sin, because they are no longer sinners. Sinners sit on the throne of their own lives. Christians get off the throne and give it back to Jesus.

> So you also must consider yourselves dead to sin and alive to God in Christ Jesus. Let not sin therefore reign in your mortal body, to make you obey its passions. Do not present your members to sin as instruments for unrighteousness, but present yourselves to God as those who have been brought from death to life, and your members to God as instruments for righteousness. For sin will have no dominion over you, since you are not under law but under grace. (Romans 6:11-14)

When you accept God's love for you in Christ, you change. You might start to hate what you used to love. The way you thought about sex, money, gender, power, the rich, the poor, politics, and a whole set of other things will change too. All your opinions on those matters probably aren't exactly Jesus' opinions yet. But when you love him, you start to see things his way. Sometimes that's fast, sometime slow. But it's always happening. Nothing's off limits. No one gets to opt out. If you come to Christ, he gets the right to change everything about you.

Jesus said, "If you love me, keep my commandments. You are my friends if you do what I've commanded you." (John 14:15, 15:14) That's how Christian obedience works. Grace, gratitude, and growth – in that order. So repent, receive his gracious love, and allow him to change you. Truth, grace, change.

> **Read Ephesians 4:17-5:21. What areas of your life aren't currently under Jesus' lordship? Are you willing to follow Jesus with your body, money, attitude, sexuality, and everything else?**
> _____
> _____
> _____

A NEW MISSION

Pursuing Jesus isn't exactly like hunting for a treasure. Once you dig up gold, you've got it. In our case, our treasure moves. Once we've got him, he says, "Great, now come follow me." Jesus is going – he's on a mission.

> *[I have come to] seek and to save the lost. (Luke 19:10)*

> *For God did not send his Son into the world to condemn the world, but in order that the world might be saved through him. (John 3:17)*

> *I came that they may have life and have it abundantly ... And this is eternal life, that they know you the only true God, and Jesus Christ whom you have sent. (John 10:10, 17:3)*

Jesus' mission can be summed up like this: to seek the lost (us), save them, and bring them into an unending, life-filled relationship with God. If this was Jesus' mission, and we follow Jesus, then this becomes our mission too. That is, if we follow God, that means following him out of the church, onto the street, into the airplane, across the ocean, and into the tribe. We follow him out of the church, across the street, and into the home. We follow him out of the church, into the office, and across the hall to the next cubicle. His mission wasn't just to show saving grace to me, but to show saving grace to others through me.

> *All authority in heaven and on earth has been given to me. Go therefore and make disciples of all nations, baptizing them in the name of the Father and of the Son and of the Holy Spirit, teaching them to observe all that I have commanded you. And behold, I am with you always, to the end of the age. (Matthew 28:18-20)*

Go.

Christianity is not simply about sermons, studies, and songs. It's about the sweat and sacrifice of missions. This Great Commission given to us by Jesus is very much like his Great Commandment,

Chapter Seven – Being

You shall love the Lord your God with all your heart and with all your soul and with all your strength and with all your mind, and your neighbor as yourself. (Luke 10:27)

When Jesus was asked what was the most important commandment of all, his answer was striking. He gave one answer with two aims – love God with everything, and love others in the same way. Jesus connected love for God with love for others. Why? Loving God means loving what He loves, and he loves not just us but our neighbor as well. If we treasure him, then we must treasure them. If we love God, then we love to make disciples.[130]

How can we possibly claim to follow God and not care about the millions of people who don't know him? He loves them. You should know this, because if you're a Christian, you used to be them. We must show the world the love of Jesus by going to them. This looks like kindness, feeding the poor, cleaning up the single mom's yard, fighting injustice, and meeting community needs. The biblical mandate for this is a simple one. Jesus came to help us, so we go to help them.

The idea is simple. God is a missionary – he left Heaven, put on flesh, and came to a particular time, place, and people – all to bring us the good news of his Kingdom. God's great mission trip is what we read about at the beginning of John's gospel:

And the Word became flesh and dwelt among us, and we have seen his glory, glory as of the only Son from the Father, full of grace and truth. (John 1:14)

Jesus became like us to bring God to us and to bring us to God. If God loved us like a missionary, then we're to do the same.

The gospel is good news that must also be proclaimed. The word gospel comes from a Greek word, *euangelion*. This is where we get the word *evangelism* – to tell the good news.

The nature of the news affects how we feel about telling it. When a couple has a new baby, they are overcome with joy and tell everyone. Why? Because having a baby is good news, and good news demands to be shared. Bad news often works just the opposite way. While the nightly news often portrays bad news everywhere, individuals rarely do this. If you and I experience something negative, like getting laid off, being abused in a relationship, or watching our parents divorce, we don't tell many people. Why? Because it's bad news, and bad news is frequently kept personal by those who don't wish to air their dirty laundry in public.

If this is true, why do so many Christians treat the gospel as though it were bad news? Many of us are terrified of telling anyone the gospel story. We are much more likely to go and serve soup at the local shelter than we are to spend an hour on the university campus striking up conversations to proclaim the gospel. Why is this? Fear.

Today it is considered intolerant, rude, and arrogant to proclaim the gospel. Many Christians respond to this cultural attitude by withholding the news of their savior, in an effort not to offend. Fueled by a fear of what people may think and a culture that says they don't want to hear it, we simply shut our mouths. We console ourselves with the mantra, "I wouldn't want to offend anyone," and we fool ourselves into believing two lies. First, that this cultural moment in which we live is uniquely resistant to the gospel, and second, that it is unloving to share news that might offend others.

Penn Jillette, Vegas comedian and no friend of religion himself remarked:

---

[130] No one that I've met or heard of understands the importance of discipleship – following Jesus and fishing for men – like Steve Murrell. His book *Wikichurch* is a helpful resource on this matter, and I highly recommend it.

I've always said that I don't respect people who don't [evangelize]. I don't respect that at all. If you believe that there's a heaven and a hell, and people could be going to hell or not getting eternal life, and you think that it's not really worth telling them this because it would make it socially awkward ... how much do you have to hate somebody to not [evangelize]? How much do you have to hate somebody to believe everlasting life is possible and not tell them that? I mean, if I believed, beyond the shadow of a doubt, that a truck was coming at you, and you didn't believe that truck was bearing down on you, there is a certain point where I tackle you. And this is more important than that.[131]

It is not love which withholds the gospel for the sake of social status. Love extends, even if it costs. Love speaks, even when few wish to hear. Love goes, even when the world wants us to stay put.

Read 2 Timothy 4:1-5. What did Paul encourage Timothy to do? What did he tell him to expect?

_____
_____
_____

A NEW POWER

The Scriptures promise that Jesus will be with us (Matt. 28:20), and even send the Holy Spirit to empower us as we go with him on mission.

But the Helper, the Holy Spirit, whom the Father will send in my name, he will teach you all things and bring to your remembrance all that I have said to you. (John 14:26)

Just before his return to Heaven, Jesus gave us the Great Commission. We just read about it. "Go make disciples..." But, after he said that, he also said, "Wait."

Wait for what? Why would Jesus tell his disciples to wait before proclaiming to the world that Jesus is alive? They needed to wait because unless the Holy Spirit empowered their proclamation, nothing would happen. They didn't just need news, they needed power. If the empowerment of the Holy Spirit was this important to Jesus, then it should be important to us. It is the Holy Spirit who enables our repentance, sanctifies us, and gives us power to do the mission of God. It is the Holy Spirit who is at work in us even before we are conscious of our own belief in him. The Holy Spirit is our helper, our guide, and the one who gives us the power to proclaim and demonstrate the good news of the gospel.

---

[131] How Much Do You Have to Hate Somebody to Not Proselytize?. http://thegospelcoalition.org/blogs/justintaylor/2009/11/17/how-much-do-you-have-to-hate-somebody-to-not-proselytize/ (accessed October 1, 2013)

Chapter Seven – Being

One role of Holy Spirit is to give gifts to God's people. These gifts range from seemingly normal gifts to some rather abnormal ones. The common thread is that they are all meant to bear witness to the gospel and bring honor to God. Jesus explains this when he says,

> *But you will receive power when the Holy Spirit has come upon you, and you will be my witnesses in Jerusalem and in all Judea and Samaria, and to the end of the earth. (Acts 1:8)*

Not only have we been given the car, but a lifetime supply of the most efficient, performance-enhancing fuel. We've been given the promise that if we ask, the Holy Spirit will empower us to do all that Jesus has given us to do, for our joy and for his glory.

The gifting of the Holy Spirit was wonderfully portrayed by C.S. Lewis in *The Chronicles of Narnia*. In the story, Narnia was overtaken by a white witch who made it always winter, but never Christmas. But when Aslan began to invade the witch's realm, Father Christmas came and gave the story's heroes gifts for their coming task of defeating the witch and establishing a new kingdom. Similarly, our world is wintered by the brokenness of sin. God does not send us into the winter without provisions.

So what must we do to get these gifts? Ask. We trust that God is good, and then we ask our good God for good gifts.

> *If you then, who are evil, know how to give good gifts to your children, how much more will the heavenly Father give the Holy Spirit to those who ask him! (Luke 11:13)*

> *Now there are varieties of gifts, but the same Spirit; and there are varieties of service, but the same Lord; and there are varieties of activities, but it is the same God who empowers them all in everyone. To each is given the manifestation of the Spirit for the common good. For to one is given through the Spirit the utterance of wisdom, and to another the utterance of knowledge according to the same Spirit, to another faith by the same Spirit, to another gifts of healing by the one Spirit, to another the working of miracles, to another prophecy, to another the ability to distinguish between spirits, to another various kinds of tongues, to another the interpretation of tongues. All these are empowered by one and the same Spirit, who apportions to each one individually as he wills. (1 Corinthians 12:4-11)*

> *[T]he fruit of the Spirit is love, joy, peace, patience, kindness, goodness, faithfulness, gentleness, self-control. (Galatians 5:22-23)*

In our day, we can read verses like these as though they were lines from fairytales. Healing? Miracles? A Spirit who lives in our hearts? How could we believe in such things? But imagine for a moment that the whole story of Jesus is true. Imagine that this God who was man, really did die and really did rise. Imagine that this was the same God who spoke the world into existence. If all this is true, is it really so difficult to imagine that this same God can, through us, do some rather uncommon things too?

Please, don't allow the cynicism of the age to let you glide past these verses. They are rich with promise. If you and I ask, the Holy Spirit will fill us and empower us for our mission: to honor God and make disciples.

When the Spirit of God grows within us, brokenness shrinks. Where you were hateful, love will grow. Where you were selfish, generosity will flower. Where you were angry, joy will break through. These are the fruits of the Spirit's work in our lives, and as we become more like Jesus, then they show up in greater bunches. Does that mean we won't struggle? No. Killing the weeds of resentment and selfishness is painful but necessary for the fruits of love and life to grow.

But, the Spirit doesn't only help us live more like Jesus. He empowers us to tell others about him. Supernatural gifts like healing and prophecy, while unable to be fully explained here, are given so that others may see that what we say is true. And why not? When Jesus was preaching, his words were often verified by signs of God's Kingdom breaking into our world. Dead people woke up. Blind people started seeing. Sick people became well. And, there are still more gifts like leadership, teaching, hospitality, and administration (Romans 12:3-8). These are all distributed by the Holy Spirit for one purpose: to fuel our pursuit of God and provide power for mission

Pursue love, and earnestly desire the spiritual gifts... (1 Corinthians 14:1)

This chart illustrates what we've discussed so far. Being and becoming like Jesus is the goal of discipleship. A disciple follows Jesus and fishes for men.

Follow Jesus "Come, follow me..." (Mark 1:17a)		Fish for Men "...and I will make you fishers of men." (Mark 1:17b)	
God is Treasure "The kingdom of heaven is like treasure..." (Matt 13:44)	**God is Trajectory** "until we all attain to the unity of the faith and of the knowledge of the Son of God, to mature manhood, to the measure of the stature of the fullness of Christ..." (Eph 4:13)	**The Mission of God** "Go and make disciples of all nations..." (Matt 28:18-20)	**The Power of God** "The Holy Spirit will come upon you and you will be my witnesses in Jerusalem, Judea, Samaria, and the ends of the Earth." (Acts 1:8)

Re-read 1 Corinthians 14:1. What is keeping you from setting your heart on spiritual gifts?

___

___

___

A BECOMING LIFE

In the book of Galatians, the Apostle Paul spends a good four chapters railing against false teachers that had come into the church. Looking like wise, learned men, they started to preach, but they had a very different gospel. It was a gospel of rules, secrets, sects, and classes. He summarizes his assault on their salvation-by-trying-harder false gospel by pointing to the kind of life it produces. The fruit that an effort-centered religion can produce is pride or despair. If you try hard and achieve, you're proud. If you try hard and fail, you despair. Then, he contrasts these with the fruit of a Christian life, and the Christian life is rather becoming. Love, joy, peace – all of these mark the man or woman who is becoming more like Jesus. This is the life which has been born into the Kingdom of God and is becoming more like him.

Chapter Seven – Being

This is a great promise, and a great test. The promise is sublime: the more we ask the Holy Spirit to lead us as we follow Christ, the more we become like him. Here, life and doctrine are inseparable – if we have believed in Christ, that confession will show up in our lives. In being Christians, we will become more like Christ. Being *and* becoming.

It's a promise paid for by the Son of God and activated in our lives by the Sprit of God, all of which is by the grace of God.

But these fruits of the Spirit are also tests, measures by which we can ask, "Is my life becoming more like Jesus'?" Are you marked mostly by pride, self-destruction, anger, frustration, and brokenness? If so, the gospel offers you hope. After all, if God can raise his Son from death, can he not also transform you? He can if the gospel story becomes your story. You can be freed to be and become like Jesus. Just as in ancient Greece, your enemy has been defeated. If you believe this news, you can live free.

QUESTIONS TO CONSIDER

1. According to Mark 1:16-20, what two actions characterize a disciple of Jesus?

2. Christians treasure Christ. Do you treasure Jesus more than other things? Are you willing to sell all that you have to "buy the field?" (Matthew 13:44)

3. Read Romans 6:11-14. How should we consider ourselves? What does this mean for you practically?

4. According to Matthew 28:18-20, what is the mission given to us by Jesus?

5. What is a missionary? According to John 1:1-16, how did Jesus act like a missionary?

6. What keeps you from telling others about Jesus?

Chapter Seven – Being

7. According to John 14:26 and Acts 1:8, what is the role of the Holy Spirit in our lives?

   _____
   _____
   _____

8. Read 1 Corinthians 12-14. What is the impression you get about the relationship between the Holy Spirit, God's people, and love?

   _____
   _____

9. According to 1 Corinthians 14:1, what should we pursue? What should we desire?

   _____
   _____

SCRIPTURE

Matthew 13:44-45
Matthew 28:18-20
John 14:26

Psalm 42
Mark 1:16-20
1 Corinthians 12-14

Ephesians 1
Matthew 22:36-40
Acts 1:8

CHAPTER EIGHT

CHURCH

Chapter Eight – Church

WHAT IS CHURCH?

In the last chapter, we read Mark 1:16-20. If you recall, Jesus was walking by the Sea of Galilee and called his first disciples saying, "Come follow me and I will make you fishers of men." Therefore, a disciple is a follower of Jesus and a fisher of men. Sounds simple.

But disciples of Jesus don't just follow him and fish for men. They do those things in spiritual family.[132] There was no option to follow Jesus all by yourself. When Jesus called Peter, he called him alongside a lot of other people. It wasn't just Jesus and Peter, or Jesus and John. It was Jesus and Peter *and* John – and all the other disciples too. Being called by Jesus meant being called into a family. Today we call that family the church.

For some, church has the nasty associations of that dreaded beast, organized religion. Did you feel the tremble go down your spine? To be fair to those with church reservations, one can certainly point to ways where the church hasn't been all it was supposed to be. When church leaders break the trust of their people by acting immorally, paying themselves outlandish salaries, or becoming political hacks for the right or the left, they lose credibility as the higher voice of God's words to the culture.

The fact remains, however, that following Christ is not merely an individual activity. Christians are individuals in community, and members of a family called the Church. Church (with a capital "C") is that group of men and women from across all time, all cultures, all races, all classes, and all people for whom Jesus has become savior. This historic reality is ensconced in the Apostle's Creed, the oldest of the creeds, saying … *I believe in the holy catholic church* … This is not speaking of the church over which the Pope rules, but the one, singular, universal church of God's people. And, if you're a follower of Jesus then you are a member of that Church.

In fact, the very word that we translate church comes from a root that means, "called out ones." So if Jesus has called you to follow him, then he's also called you to be a part of his Church.

Yet, that one, universal Church of all believers from all time has smaller, local expressions. And it is your association with that smaller, local expression which can make or break your relationship with God and your effectiveness on mission. In short, your doctrine of church will deeply affect your life.

Belonging to a group of Church is not an option, but it is a privilege. Nowhere in the New Testament do we find any Christians operating outside the context of spiritual family. Why? Because it is everywhere assumed that you and I and everyone else who follows Jesus will joyfully follow him with others. True, your relationship with Jesus is your responsibility. But, you cannot say, "I love Jesus but don't like his Church." Those are tough words for Jesus to hear, since the church is also pictured as Jesus' bride. I can't imagine someone saying to me, "I love you, but your wife I don't really care for." If you have a problem with my wife, then I've got a problem with you!

The Scriptures give many metaphors of church, a few of which we'll discuss further here: a spiritual family, a diverse family, a countercultural family, a serving family, a generous family, and a missional family.

---

[132] I'm grateful to Steve Murrell for this observation.

> **What is your history with church? What has been good? What concerns do you have regarding church?**
> _____
> _____
> _____

A SPIRITUAL FAMILY

Relationship with Jesus means relationship with God's family. Jesus taught us to say to God, "Our Father, who is in heaven…" (Matt. 6:9, Lk. 11:2). In fact, calling God "Father" is a sign that we're his kids – his adopted children.[133] The writer of Hebrews is even more explicit about this, reminding us that Jesus is now pleased to call us brothers and sisters.[134] What an amazing idea! In Christ, we are adopted into the family of God, with God as our Father and Jesus as our great elder brother.

Now, we're no longer just a group of people who see each other in a building on Sunday. Neither is the church a "them" and "us" thing. Now, there is only us. All across the New Testament we see this. Paul, once an enemy of the church and a murderer of Christians, experienced adoption into God's family. Formerly a murderer, after his conversion he was given the title "brother."

This is scandalous. If a man walked into my church, arrested my leaders, and led the lynching of one of them, I must admit that it would be hard for me to call him brother a few months later. But, that's exactly what happened to the church in Jerusalem, because that's what the gospel does. It doesn't just make enemies friends, it makes them family.

Because we've been reconciled to God by grace, we must reconcile to one another.

Jesus has given the church a few practices to remind us of our membership in his family. Every church that belongs to Jesus does them, because Jesus did and asked us to as well. The first of these is baptism. Before beginning his ministry, Jesus met John, his cousin, at the Jordan River.

> *Then Jesus came from Galilee to the Jordan to John, to be baptized by him. John would have prevented him, saying, "I need to be baptized by you, and do you come to me?" But Jesus answered him, "Let it be so now, for thus it is fitting for us to fulfill all righteousness." Then he consented. And when Jesus was baptized, immediately he went up from the water, and behold, the heavens were opened to him, and he saw the*

---

[133] *For you did not receive the spirit of slavery to fall back into fear, but you have received the Spirit of adoption as sons, by whom we cry, "Abba! Father!" The Spirit himself bears witness with our spirit that we are children of God, and if children, then heirs–heirs of God and fellow heirs with Christ…* (Rom. 8:15-17a)

[134] *For he who sanctifies and those who are sanctified all have one source. That is why [Jesus] is not ashamed to call them brothers…* (Heb. 2:11).

Chapter Eight – Church

> *Spirit of God descending like a dove and coming to rest on him; and behold, a voice from heaven said, "This is my beloved Son, with whom I am well pleased."* (Matthew 3:13-17)

Notice how immediately after Jesus was baptized, God the Father declared his sonship to the world. This should signal something to us, namely that baptism is connected to our adoption into the family of God. What is baptism? It is a physical act with a deep spiritual significance, where one is immersed in water to symbolize being cleansed of sin. In being baptized, Jesus humbled himself to set an example for us. When we become baptized, we remember what Jesus has done to bring us from death to life, and show everyone watching that we now belong to God's family.

The second practice that Jesus left his church is the Eucharist, or Communion. In an interesting symmetry, this came at the end of his ministry, where baptism was given at the beginning. On the night before his crucifixion, Jesus showed us this practice:

> *Now as they were eating, Jesus took bread, and after blessing it broke it and gave it to the disciples, and said, "Take, eat; this is my body." And he took a cup, and when he had given thanks he gave it to them, saying, "Drink of it, all of you, for this is my blood of the covenant, which is poured out for many for the forgiveness of sins. I tell you I will not drink again of this fruit of the vine until that day when I drink it new with you in my Father's kingdom."* (Matthew 26:26-29)

Again, notice the connection to family. Jesus is saying to his guys, "When you eat this bread and drink this wine, remember me and the new covenant of grace, purchased by my blood. I won't drink this again until we are together, as one family, in my Father's kingdom." If baptism is a sacrament which looks back to our salvation, communion is one which looks forward to the coming of God's kingdom – his covenant family.

You and I can belong to the family of God. I suppose that's why it's called the Eucharist. That word comes from a Greek word, *eucharisteo*, meaning, "I give thanks." Being adopted into the church – the family of God – is definitely something to be thankful for.

What are the two sacraments of the church? What do they mean?
_____
_____
_____

A DIVERSE FAMILY

Church is pictured many ways in the Scriptures. It's called the body of Christ,[135] a holy people,[136] and even the family of God.[137]

The call to follow Jesus always means doing so with others. Once we embrace this idea, then we open ourselves up to a beautiful reality – the multifaceted, diverse, spiritual family that is Jesus' Church. After coming to follow Jesus, the disciples found themselves thrown into a new family – a spiritual one. The beauty of this diversity is expressed eloquently by Paul:

> *For just as the body is one and has many members, and all the members of the body, though many, are one body, so it is with Christ … For the body does not consist of one member but of many. If the foot should say, "Because I am not a hand, I do not belong to the body," that would not make it any less a part of the body. And if the ear should say, "Because I am not an eye, I do not belong to the body," that would not make it any less a part of the body. If the whole body were an eye, where would be the sense of hearing? If the whole body were an ear, where would be the sense of smell? But as it is, God arranged the members in the body, each one of them, as he chose. If all were a single member, where would the body be? As it is, there are many parts, yet one body. The eye cannot say to the hand, "I have no need of you," nor again the head to the feet, "I have no need of you." … Now you are the body of Christ and individually members of it. (1 Corinthians 12:12, 14-21, 27).*

Bodies need many different parts to work properly. Therefore, so does the church – the body of Christ. This has two implications. First, we cannot have too low a view of ourselves. Some Christians spend their lives trying to be something they are not. Wishing they were different, they are plagued with jealousy. Christian community must be different. Each disciple of Jesus Christ has a role to fill, a place to fit. We can't be so preoccupied with wishing we were different than we are that we never find our fit. If God made you (which he did), then he made you for a purpose. One of these is to fit in the body of Christ.

Second, we can't have so high a view of ourselves that we undervalue others who are different than us. You and I don't have the luxury of preferring people like us. If I'm going to be a true part of the body of Christ, then I must recognize the diversity of gifting, backgrounds, similarities, and differences and celebrate them. The reality is simple: I cannot be a real disciple of Jesus without other disciples. I need them, and they need me. I need their strength to shore up my weaknesses. I need their backgrounds to keep me from seeing selfishly. We need spiritual mothers, fathers, brothers and sisters, even sons and daughters. And, they cannot all look the same as us.

Christians must beware the temptation to draw near to each other on the basis of mere affinity. That is how everyone in the world lives. We are called to gather not on the basis of our color, our background, our bank statements, or our hobbies. We are called to walk together as a diverse, spiritual family with bonds deeper than affinity and roots stronger than preference. We are called to love past differences and even offenses, and in so doing to demonstrate the love of the one who has loved us.

---

[135] *…so we, though many, are one body in Christ, and individually members one of another. (Rom. 12:5)*

[136] *But you are a chosen race, a royal priesthood, a holy nation, a people for his own possession, that you may proclaim the excellencies of him who called you out of darkness into his marvelous light, (1 Pet. 2:9)*

[137] *So then you are no longer strangers and aliens, but you are fellow citizens with the saints and members of the household of God, (Eph. 2:19)*

Chapter Eight – Church

> *For as in one body we have many members, and the members do not all have the same function, so we, though many, are one body in Christ, and individually members one of another. Having gifts that differ according to the grace given to us, let us use them... (Romans 12:4-6a)*

Paul isn't saying that we should merely celebrate church diversity. He says that we're dependent upon it. I often tell my church, "We need you, and you need us." We are, as Paul says, members of one another. This is an uncomfortable, countercultural way to live. But if you've ever seen it in real life, it is really beautiful.

We simply cannot hope to pursue Jesus Christ alone. We must find ourselves in a church which is centered on this gospel story. And, one of the hallmarks of a gospel-centered church is its diversity. How do I know? Because that's what the church at the end of time looks like. In the vision of Revelation, John describes the worshippers of God at the end of the age. Searching for words to describe the breathtaking picture he saw, he said this:

> *After this I looked, and behold, a great multitude that no one could number, from every nation, from all tribes and peoples and languages, standing before the throne and before the Lamb, clothed in white robes, with palm branches in their hands, and crying out with a loud voice, "Salvation belongs to our God who sits on the throne, and to the Lamb!" And all the angels were standing around the throne and around the elders and the four living creatures, and they fell on their faces before the throne and worshiped God, saying, "Amen! Blessing and glory and wisdom and thanksgiving and honor and power and might be to our God forever and ever! Amen." (Revelation 7:9-12)*

That phrase, "every nation," leaves no room for debate. It literally means all ethnolinguistic people groups. All of them will be represented in the future worship of God. Heaven isn't a white traditional church. It's not an African church. It's not a black, gospel church. It's not a Chinese house church. Heaven's worship is the loud cries of joy lifted up before God in every language, from every people group, across all time. Wouldn't it be something if our local churches looked a little bit like that?

The reality is simple. I can't be the man I'm called to be without the church. I'm grateful that our church is marked by such a spirit. As I look across our gatherings, I see different colors, different backgrounds, different ages, and different gifts, and I find it beautiful.

Read Ephesians 2:11-16. What implications does this have for your understanding of church?

_____
_____
_____

Church – **Chapter Eight**

A COUNTERCULTURAL FAMILY

Because the church is the family of God, its culture is different than the world around it. Jesus taught us to pray, "Father … let your kingdom come, and your will be done." In asking for this, Jesus is teaching us to pray for a Heavenly reality to become our earthly reality. The church, then, should be an outpost of this new kingdom. And, in the Kingdom of God, sex, money, power, love – all of life is approached differently. So, the church should be a kingdom outpost, living out a kingdom counterculture.

> *But you are a chosen race, a royal priesthood, a holy nation, a people for his own possession, that you may proclaim the excellencies of him who called you out of darkness into his marvelous light. Once you were not a people, but now you are God's people … (1 Peter 2:9-10a)*

The church is God's handpicked people, called to live as his family. And his family gets the privilege of showing forth his excellence in every area of life. Like a colony of new life, the people of God are meant to embody the culture, values, story, and mission of our "Heavenly country." We are not to so assimilate into our host culture that we lose our distinctiveness. In fact, we are to live so distinctly different lives that our host culture moves toward us.

Consider the words of Jesus:

> *If the world hates you, know that it has hated me before it hated you. If you were of the world, the world would love you as its own; but because you are not of the world, but I chose you out of the world, therefore the world hates you. (John 15:18-19).*

According to this section, in what ways should the church be different than the host culture? Why?
_____
_____
_____

A GENEROUS FAMILY

The early church was marked by extreme generosity.

> *And they devoted themselves to the apostles' teaching and the fellowship, to the breaking of bread and the prayers. And awe[e] came upon every soul, and many wonders and signs were being done through the apostles. And all who believed were together and had all things in common. And they were selling their*

Chapter Eight – Church

> *possessions and belongings and distributing the proceeds to all, as any had need. And day by day, attending the temple together and breaking bread in their homes, they received their food with glad and generous hearts, praising God and having favor with all the people. And the Lord added to their number day by day those who were being saved. (Acts 2:42-47)*

The church in Jerusalem was so transformed by the gospel that their approach to money totally changed. Because they now had been reconciled to God, they already possessed true riches. Therefore, they were free to share their earthly ones. This is what happens in the church – the grace of God becomes more precious to us than money, breaking our attachment to it.

Is it wrong to have money? No. Is it wrong to love it more than God and others? Absolutely. Paul reminds us that, "the love of money is the root of all kinds of evils." (1 Tim. 6:10) Think of all the evil that happens in the world all because different interests, people, and governments are trying to control money. This approach to money should be challenged on every level by the church, because the church has a kingdom value – generosity.

> *The point is this: Whoever sows sparingly will also reap sparingly, and whoever sows bountifully will also reap bountifully. Each man must give as he has decided in his heart, not reluctantly or under compulsion, for God loves a cheerful giver. And God is able to make all grace abound to you, so that having all sufficiency in all things at all times, you may abound in every good work.*
> *(2 Corinthians 9:6-8)*

God promises to meet our needs, even as we are cheerfully generous to others. In short, if the church's doctrine says that God's been generous, then the church's life should show off such radical generosity. Money is neither good nor bad, it is a tool. We can either build the kingdom of God with it through acts of generosity, or the kingdom of self through acts of selfishness. In the church, however, radical generosity should be the norm that newcomers experience time after time.

> *And God is able to make all grace abound to you, so that having all sufficiency in all things at all times, you may abound in every good work. (2 Corinthians 9:8).*

What worries do you have about money? How does this section help you?
_____
_____
_____

A SERVING FAMILY

No one exemplifies a kingdom approach to power more than Jesus. In John 13, we read an amazing account of the Son of God humbling himself to serve his disciples.

It was the night before he was to go the cross. Jesus, as you might imagine, had been thinking about this evening for a long time. Repeatedly, he tried to tell his disciples what was going on, and repeatedly they didn't understand. They thought their Messiah would be a warrior king who would kill all God's enemies. Jesus came from a Kingdom culture of loving service, and these two cultures were clashing. The disciples had begun to argue a bit. "I think I'll be greatest in the kingdom," one said. The others scoffed, "You? Please." The arguing continued. Jesus, watching his people, his future church, miss it again, got up from the table. Slowly, he walked to the water basin and filled it with water. As the disciples were arguing, he approached one, knelt down, and removed his sandals.

The room fell silent. Forgetting about their argument, the disciples watched as the man they believed was God the Son, the Messiah, washed the dirt, manure, and grime off their feet with his own hands. One by one, Jesus washed them. They looked on, stunned, as their master did a job fit for the lowest of slaves. When it came to Peter's turn, he spoke up, "No, Lord. You cannot do this." But Jesus persisted, telling him that unless he was washed by Jesus, he couldn't be truly clean. After he was finished, Jesus said:

> *Do you understand what I have done to you? You call me Teacher and Lord, and you are right, for so I am. If I then, your Lord and Teacher, have washed your feet, you also ought to wash one another's feet. For I have given you an example, that you also should do just as I have done to you.* (John 13:12-15)

The disciples had never seen this before. In fact, the world had never seen this before. Powerful people had slaves, servants, armies, and certainly never washed anyone's feet. But, Jesus' approach to power is totally different than ours. The church, therefore, is to be a living, breathing example of the servant leadership of Jesus Christ.

The leaders of God's church aren't there to be served by God's people, like little CEOs. They are there to serve God's people, like little Christs. The point of this service is simple: so that the church will be strengthened, built together in love.

> *And he gave the apostles, the prophets, the evangelists, the shepherds and teachers, to equip the saints for the work of ministry, for building up the body of Christ, until we all attain to the unity of the faith and of the knowledge of the Son of God, to mature manhood, to the measure of the stature of the fullness of Christ, so that we may no longer be children, tossed to and fro by the waves and carried about by every wind of doctrine, by human cunning, by craftiness in deceitful schemes. Rather, speaking the truth in love, we are to grow up in every way into him who is the head, into Christ, from whom the whole body, joined and held together by every joint with which it is equipped, when each part is working properly, makes the body grow so that it builds itself up in love.* (Ephesians 4:11-16).

In the church, there is certainly order. God made sure that his people were not without proper leaders. But these leaders aren't the kind of people we might imagine. We want leaders with great degrees, broad skill sets, and charismatic charm. God, on the other hand, has different requirements.

Chapter Eight – Church

> *The saying is trustworthy: If anyone aspires to the office of overseer, he desires a noble task. Therefore an overseer must be above reproach, the husband of one wife, sober-minded, self-controlled, respectable, hospitable, able to teach, not a drunkard, not violent but gentle, not quarrelsome, not a lover of money. He must manage his own household well, with all dignity keeping his children submissive, for if someone does not know how to manage his own household, how will he care for God's church? He must not be a recent convert, or he may become puffed up with conceit and fall into the condemnation of the devil. Moreover, he must be well thought of by outsiders, so that he may not fall into disgrace, into a snare of the devil.*
> (1 Timothy 3:1-7).

God's word teaches that the church is to be led by elders[138] – certain men of God chosen for their character, love for others, graciousness as fathers and husbands, ability to teach God's word, and track records as followers of Christ. Nowhere on that list is charisma, charm, or a great seminary degree. In fact, most of these qualifications are character qualities, not skills. What does this mean? It means that the leaders of God's church are to approach power the same way Jesus did: through sacrificial service to others. These men are assisted in their task by deacons – men and women of God who serve through a variety of means.

If God – the greatest leader – can humble himself to wash the dirt off our feet, then God's leaders must.

How should Christian leadership be different than worldly leadership? Why?
_____
_____
_____

A MISSIONAL FAMILY

Jesus people are invited onto Jesus' mission.

> *Go therefore and make disciples of all nations, baptizing them in the name of the Father, and of the Son, and the Holy Spirit, teaching them to observe all that I have commanded you. And behold, I am with you always, to the end of age.* (Matthew 28:18-20)

Just before his ascension, Jesus gave a Great Commission to his church. He did not come to inaugurate a static group of people. He came to ignite a dynamic, missional movement – to recover what was lost in the garden. The good news of the Jesus story is that in Jesus everything can be made new. The lost are saved, the hurting healed, and the world renewed.

---

[138] Elders in the scripture point to the office of pastor in the modern day church. The NT uses three words to describe this role: elder, pastor, and overseer. These three words form three different perspectives on a central office, that of the elder/pastor of the local church congregation.

God rescues his people for a purpose. And the purpose isn't really about us. From the beginning, God has been consumed with a passion to share the greatness of his glory with his creatures. Human sin and rebellion broke that fellowship. But Christ has come to heal the divide between God and humanity, and has given the mission of sharing that good news to only one group: the church. Any gathering of people who call themselves a church and aren't consumed with this passion aren't the church! A social group, maybe. A religious charity, perhaps. But not the church.

My friend Dr. Rice Broocks sums it up this way:

> *Everyone who is saved, baptized, and filled with the Holy Spirit today should also be added to a local church. The church is God's instrument for advancing his Kingdom. He has no plan B. The church is the only legitimate setting for walking out the Christian faith. All who truly desire to follow Christ will find their place in a church family.*[139]

No plan B. This can be kind of surprising, given the quirky, awkward, stumbling nature of churches. God has chosen this ragtag, grace-saved bunch of nobodies to display the wisdom and the riches of this doctrine: the gospel. He's taken the messed up, the poor, the hurting, the shamed, the different, and all who have been a victim of their own foolishness and rescued them.

All this means is that in the Kingdom of God, life is lived uniquely. Churches are to be unique communities of love, life and transformation, within their larger communities. Jesus himself even said that if we were his, the world around us would notice just by the way we love and take care of one another.[140]

If we're going to take Jesus' commands with any degree of seriousness, then we've got to notice the fact that this command wasn't uttered to each individual disciple. This was the command to the lot of them – the church. The mission of the master has become the mission of the master's people. It's the church's duty and delight to participate with God on this great adventure of watching the good news of the gospel not merely to take root in the hearts of her own people, but transform the lives of people in communities, cities, and across the world. You can't do that. I can't do that. But we – we must.

What is the mission of the church?

_____
_____
_____

---

[139] Rice Broocks and Steve Murrell, *The Purple Book: Biblical Foundations.* Grand Rapids, MI: Zondervan, 2008, 40.

[140] John 13:35

Chapter Eight – Church

DON'T GO ALONE

One of the great lies of our cultural moment is that we can be who we're supposed be all on our own. This kind of thinking is completely absent from the biblical vision. This is why church – true, godly, deep community with all its warts and problems – is so crucial. I simply cannot be who God calls me to be alone. Neither can you. This is probably what Paul meant when the Spirit inspired these words in him, "So we, though many, are one body in Christ, and individually members one of another." (Rom. 12:5) Men and women of God need one another.

Church is certainly not perfect. When people show up, problems will. However, it can be authentic, composed of men and women who gather because of the gospel of the grace of Jesus Christ. My own experience bears this out. Once I connected, once I served, once I stopped looking for a way out, once I stopped being flaky in my attendance, once I looked at the men and women occupying the seats next to me as precious to God and vital to my growth, then I grew. It was, for me, the difference between renting and owning. Renters use a house, owners invest in a house. Renters stay until a better deal comes along, owners sink their life savings into making their home the best one possible. I had to stop renting the church. I had to become an owner.

Like a great experiment, church can be a petri dish for the culture of a new Kingdom to germinate, replicate, and grow. It can actually become a community into which the world may peer and say, "Wow, I didn't know people could live that way." Church is not meant to be different than the world in spite of the world, but for the sake of the world that God is coming back to redeem. For their sake, then, we come together as the church – for the glory of God and the good of all people.

How about you? Are you a church renter or a church owner? Why?

_____
_____
_____

QUESTIONS TO CONSIDER

1. Read Ephesians 5:25-27. How did Jesus serve the church?

2. According to Romans 8:15-17, what kind of spirit did we receive when we believed? If God is our Father, then who are our brothers and sisters?

3. Read 1 Corinthians 12:12-27. What does this tell us about the importance of diversity in the church? Does this encourage you? Why?

4. According to Romans 12:4-6, what is our relationship to each other within the church?

5. Read Revelation 7:9-12. Who is before the throne of God? What does that mean for church?

Chapter Eight – Church

6. Read Micah 3:11 and 2 Corinthians 9:6-8. Are you being faithful with money? Are you generous to the church and to others? What is God's promise related to money, according to these verses?

   _____
   _____
   _____

7. According to Acts 2:42-47, how did the early church treat money? What do you think fueled such extreme generosity?

   _____
   _____
   _____

8. How should leadership look different in the church than anywhere else?

   _____
   _____
   _____

9. Read Ephesians 4:11-12. What is the job of the leaders in the church (the Pastors, etc)?

   _____
   _____

10. According to 1 Timothy 3:1-7, what are the qualifications for leadership in the church?

    _____
    _____

11. What is the mission of the church, according to Matthew 28:18-20? Why does this matter?

    _____
    _____

12. Is church important to you? Why?

    _____
    _____

Church — **Chapter Eight**

SCRIPTURE

Ephesians 5:25-27

Matthew 3:13-17

Acts 2:42-47

1 Timothy 3:1-7

1 Corinthians 11:17-34

Ephesians 4:11-16

Romans 12:1-8

Matthew 28:18-20

2 Corinthians 9:6-8

CHAPTER NINE

HOPE

Chapter Nine – Hope

THE FUTURE IS COMING

If the Christian story were music, it would be a symphony in four parts: creation, fall, redemption, and consummation. So far we've given eight chapters to exploring the first three movements. This final chapter will consider the last movement, the future consummation.

Consummation refers to moment when Heaven and Earth are reunited in a lasting embrace, never to be separated by sin again. Remember, the Christian story is a *story*, and stories – like great pieces of music – have a final resolution. The future is coming. And since it is coming, we should aim to understand what God has told us about it and how we should live now.

Perhaps you've heard someone describe one who thinks about the end of days with the moniker, "He's so heavenly minded that he's no earthly good." Hedging his bets that Jesus is coming any second now, he doesn't pay much attention to things in this life. He's not concerned with developing his career, deepening relationships, stewarding the environment, or building a long term project. Why would he? Won't the whole thing just get crumpled up in the wastebasket of history anyway? Isn't the judgment going to just wipe the whole thing out?

Thinking like this has crept into mainstream Christian minds in the last century or two. Fueled by a fundamentalistic desire to get out of here and on to the sweet by-and-by, Christian publishers have littered the shelves with every kind of book on the end of the world that you could possibly imagine. This leads to two twin errors. On the one side are those Christians who have become so obsessed with the any-minute return of Christ that they're utterly odd and almost useless. In the other ditch are those who are either scared of the future or annoyed by the rapture zealotry they've seen, so they just forget about it altogether. We should neither be obsessed with nor flippant about the future. Seeking to understand what God has promised, we should live wisely in hopeful anticipation of it.

CONSUMMATION CONFUSION

One's view of the end of things is deeply tied to one's view of the beginning of things. If you believe that life is the product of an accidental collocation of atoms, as famous atheist Bertrand Russell once said, then you'll have no problem accepting that death is the end. This is the view of naturalism. Friedrich Nietzsche sums up this view of things well when he wrote this:

> *Once upon a time, in some out of the way corner of that universe which is dispersed into numberless twinkling solar systems, there was a star upon which clever beasts invented knowing. That was the most arrogant and mendacious minute of "world history," but nevertheless, it was only a minute. After nature had drawn a few breaths, the star cooled and congealed, and the clever beasts had to die. One might invent such a fable, and yet he still would not have adequately illustrated how miserable, how shadowy and transient, how aimless and arbitrary the human intellect looks within nature. There were eternities*

> *during which it did not exist. And when it is all over with the human intellect, nothing will have happened.*[141]

Feeling encouraged yet? While it may be convenient to embrace such a worldview at some points, it seems to come at a very high cost – the cost of any hope whatsoever.

However, naturalism is not the only worldview on the market. As previously mentioned (in chapter three) there are some who believe that this world and everything in it are really quite divine. So the point of things is to come to terms with that fact – that we're all really part of one final, fundamental substance. The more we realize that, the more we're meant to lose grip on the selfish pursuits to which we give our lives and embrace the One (sometimes called god, gaia, the universal spirit, Brahma, or something else).

On this view, there is no end of things, *per se*. That's because everything is divine. And divine things are eternal things. So the human soul is in a constant, cyclical struggle of reincarnation and reinvention to take another crack at getting this "becoming one with all things," thing down pat. Contrasting this view with the Christian understanding, Michael Horton writes:

> *[Pantheism] destroys personal existence … In losing personhood, [pantheism] also destroys community … When, as Eastern religions commonly teach, the self finally achieves its unity with all being, there is no personal consciousness of this ostensible benefit. The raindrop dissolves into an ocean of being … However, in Scripture there is no assumption that the soul is immortal. Rather, like the body, it is a created substance with a beginning and an end. Immortality was the goal held out to Adam and Eve in the Tree of Life, and not merely for the soul but for the whole person. It is this immortality that was forfeited by Adam but has been promised to those who trust in Jesus Christ.*[142]

Those who trust in Christ and have embraced the Christian story are not on an endless cycle of attempts at divinity, nor are they on a high speed train to thermodynamic heat death. Christians have hope for the future because the future has come rushing backwards into the now – into history, in fact – in the resurrection of Jesus. In that event, we see what future is *actually* coming. And it's already here, though not quite yet.

How does our view of the end of history affect how we live our lives? What strange ideas have you found yourself believing that really aren't all that biblical?

_____
_____
_____

---

[141] Friedrich Nietzsche, *Über Wahrheit und Lüge im außermoralischen Sinn* (1873), Part 1.

[142] Horton, Michael S, *The Christian Faith: A Systematic Theology for Pilgrims on the Way*

Chapter Nine – Hope

BETWEEN ALREADY AND NOT YET

How can the future be here already, but not yet? What does, "already and not yet" even mean?

One way to view the Bible is as a history of the story – what God has done along the timeline of history from creation to redemption. Taking this view, the appearing of Jesus Christ was a really big deal. In Jesus, the Kingdom of God had showed up. Why is this important? Because in the fall, humanity rebelled against God's rule and put the cosmos under the authority of another kingdom, that of God's enemy. So, when Jesus shows up at the beginning of the book of Mark and announces:

> *The time is fulfilled, and the kingdom of God is at hand; repent and believe in the gospel,* (Mark 1:15)

He's saying something cosmic, not dramatic. Jesus was saying that the kingdom of God which was ripped away from earth so long ago had come back, and the King was there making the announcement.

The Kingdom of God was inaugurated by Jesus, and will be consummated upon his return. We living in the already-but-not-yet tension between those two events.

So Jesus lives, dies, and rises. What was that all about? How did that bring about the Kingdom? N.T. Wright notes:

> *Crucifixion of a would-be Messiah meant that he wasn't the Messiah, not that he was. When Jesus was crucified, every single disciple knew what it meant: we backed the wrong horse.*
> *The game is over. Whatever their expectations, and however Jesus had been trying to redefine those expectations, as far as they were concerned hope had crumbled into ashes ... [But] resurrection was and is the defeat of death ...*[143]

In dying and rising, Jesus was giving us a picture of the future awaiting all those who would trust him by faith. We will taste death (that is, we will all physically die at some point). But like Jesus, we will rise to a future where we have bodies like his and the rift that sin has created between God and humanity, between heaven and earth, will be no more.

But of course, that's not the world we're currently living in. Our world isn't the new heavens and the new earth. Our world is still full of pain, misery, and sorrow. Despite Jesus's resurrection, there still remains an unthinkable amount of sadness and death, sorrow and depression, brokenness and pain. So what gives?

The world we're currently occupying is one that many Christian teachers describe as "between the already and the not yet." What that means is simply this: Jesus has decisively defeated sin and death on the cross. He has been victorious over sin and death in the resurrection. By faith in him, that same power will defeat sin and death in us, and through us to others. This belief showed up immediately after the resurrection of Christ. A few years afterwards, Paul wrote to the church in Ephesus that he was

---

[143] N. T. Wright. *Surprised by Hope.* 66, 89

praying for them to know the resurrection power of Christ in their own lives (Ephesians 1:15-23). Apparently for Paul, at least, the resurrection wasn't just a future event out there somewhere. It's an event that means that the future kingdom has invaded the present. So what does this mean for us?

First, it means that we can have hope for the future if we have hope in Christ. If Jesus rose physically from death, then not even death will defeat Jesus' people. We will rise like he rose. Second, this means that the world in which we live – the physical one with sweat and work, joy and pain, rain and sun – matters. Why? Because Jesus rose with a physical body. And finally, this means that no matter what we face, we have reason for powerful hope, anticipating the victory of our king which has already been won, but which has not yet been consummated in history. This means that even disease, pain, and suffering have no power over us but to serve for our growth.

We must live in the tension between the already and the not yet – living life today in light of the life to come. Sam Storms, Pastor and Theologian, explains,

> *Do we live every day with one foot lifted ever so deftly off the ground in constant alert and anxious expectation of the moment when we will depart this world and enter into the splendor of heaven and the presence of God himself? ... In this you find strength to endure trials and setbacks and disappointments. In this, says Peter, you find hope when everything else is hopeless. This glorious truth is what will sustain and empower you for everything that lies ahead.*[144]

Read 1 Corinthians 15:50-58. What does the future hold? What, according to this passage, should we do in light of the coming future?

THY KINGDOM COME

Jesus' disciples once asked him to teach them to pray. We read the account in Luke 11:

> *Now Jesus was praying in a certain place, and when he finished, one of his disciples said to him, "Lord, teach us to pray, as John taught his disciples." And he said to them, "When you pray, say: "Father, hallowed be your name. Your kingdom come... (Luke 11:1-2)*

---

[144] Storms, Sam. "Living with One Foot Raised." EnjoyingGod.com. http://www.samstorms.com/enjoying-god-blog/post/living-with-one-foot-raised (accessed May 22, 2014).

Chapter Nine – Hope

This prayer teaches us something important about how Christians are to live. We are to live as Kingdom people, looking to bring Heaven's culture, values, power, love, and message down from above and back from the future into the present time and place in which we live. The future that is coming is one where the Kingdom of God fully invades this world. That's what John saw when he wrote:

> *Then I saw a new heaven and a new earth, for the first heaven and the first earth had passed away, and the sea was no more. And I saw the holy city, new Jerusalem, coming down out of heaven from God, prepared as a bride adorned for her husband. And I heard a loud voice from the throne saying, "Behold, the dwelling place of God is with man. He will dwell with them, and they will be his people, and God himself will be with them as their God. He will wipe away every tear from their eyes, and death shall be no more, neither shall there be mourning, nor crying, nor pain anymore, for the former things have passed away." And he who was seated on the throne said, "Behold, I am making all things new." (Revelation 21:1-5)*

My aunt passed away too early in life. In her early 50s, this triathlete turned massage therapist knew what healthy physical living looked like. And then the cancer came. At first, the odds of beating it seemed good. But it grew worse and finally took her life a few years later. Before she died, I read this passage to her. It brought her hope.

For the Christian, there are great reasons and resources from which to draw hope – hope that sustains in sickness and death, and which cheerfully enjoys the pleasures of life. Praying "thy kingdom come," isn't just the repetition of a pie in the sky future. It is the mission that should occupy our prayers, fuel our hope, inform our work, and sustain our peace. In his book, *Surprised by Hope*, N.T. Wright explains:

> *As I see it, the prayer ['thy kingdom come,'] was powerfully answered at the first Easter and will finally be answered fully when heaven and earth are joined in the new Jerusalem. Easter was when Hope in person surprised the whole world by coming forward from the future into the present. The ultimate future hope remains a surprise, partly because we don't know when it will arrive and partly because at present we have only images and metaphors for it, leaving us to guess that the reality will be far greater, and more surprising, still. And the intermediate hope – the things that happen in the present time to implement Easter and anticipate the final day – are always surprising because, left to ourselves, we lapse into a kind of collusion with entropy, acquiescing in the general belief that things may be getting worse but that there's nothing much we can do about them. And we are wrong. Our task ... is to live as resurrection people in between Easter and the final day, with our Christian life, corporate and individual, in both worship and mission, as a sign of the first and a foretaste of the second.*[145]

The Bible doesn't teach Christians to look forward to the day God takes us away from this world. Rather, we are to look forward to the moment when Heaven and Earth are brought back together, never to be separated again.

---

[145] N. T. Wright. *Surprised by Hope*. 54.

Read Revelation 21-22. What sticks out to you about John's vision of the ultimate future? How is it different than what you may have expected?

_____
_____
_____

IT'S GOING TO GET BETTER, AND WORSE

So what should our expectations be of the future? Some are attracted to doomsday prophecies, lamenting how the world is under a curse and destined for judgment. Still others seem utterly preoccupied with creating heaven here on earth, blissfully unaware that on our own that's not possible. If we're caught in between the already and the not yet, what should we expect?

We can note first that there are many passages in the Scriptures that teach that the future will get worse. People won't listen to the truth:

> *For the time is coming when people will not endure sound teaching, but having itching ears they will accumulate for themselves teachers to suit their own passions, and will turn away from listening to the truth and wander off into myths. (2 Timothy 4:3-4)*

War and violence will increase:

> *And you will hear of wars and rumors of wars. See that you are not alarmed, for this must take place, but the end is not yet. For nation will rise against nation, and kingdom against kingdom, and there will be famines and earthquakes in various places. All these are but the beginning of the birth pains. (Matthew 24:6-8)*

And Christians around the world will be increasingly persecuted:

> *Then they will deliver you up to tribulation and put you to death, and you will be hated by all nations for my name's sake. And then many will fall away and betray one another and hate one another. And many false prophets will arise and lead many astray. And because lawlessness will be increased, the love of many will grow cold. (Matthew 24:9-12)*

Reading verses like those don't make one feel too hopeful about the future. Approaching the end, the volume will be turned up on unrighteousness. But that's not the only thing the Bible says about the future. We're told that the gospel will and must be preached to all nations:

Chapter Nine – Hope

> *But the one who endures to the end will be saved. And this gospel of the kingdom will be proclaimed throughout the whole world as a testimony to all nations, and then the end will come. (Matthew 24:13-14)*

Though the church will endure suffering, she will prevail:

> *...on this rock I will build my church, and the gates of hell shall not prevail against it. (Matthew 16:18)*

The glory of God will cover the earth:

> *[T]he earth shall be full of the knowledge of the Lord as the waters cover the sea... (Isaiah 11:9)*

And Jesus will be with us, even in the midst of all of it:

> *...and behold, I am with you always, even to the very end of the age. (Matthew 28:20b)*

All of this taken together should make us realistic and optimistic, hopeful and human. The man or woman of God who understands what the Bible says about the future will avoid the naive optimism that most political pundits or academic idealists pedal. Because we understand human nature, we know that we'll never create utopia on earth. Filled with hope for the future, we'll also never settle for a disengaged pessimism that retreats from the world. The resurrection of Jesus tells us that God is very interested in this world. He did bleed to redeem it, after all.

How does this section shape the way you read the news?
_____
_____
_____

DEATH AND THE INTERMEDIATE STATE

The bible teaches that when we die, our spirits – that immaterial but essential part of who we are – go to be with the Lord. When Jesus was speaking to the thief on the cross next to him who believed, he told him, "today you will be with me in paradise." (Luke 23:43). Paul also taught that death in this body meant presence with Christ (Phil 1:23). This has been called the *intermediate state*. That's because a disembodied heaven is not the final destiny of those who trust in Christ, but an intermediate place of unbelievable but imperfect bliss, for those who trust in Christ.

But if we mistake this intermediate heaven for the new heavens and the new earth, then we'll misunderstand a huge point of our redemption. Jesus didn't die and rise just to keep us from hell, but to renew the whole cosmos. Horton explains:

Christian hope is oriented not to the intermediate state (going to heaven when we die), but to the renovation of creation, including our natural bodies ... The whole earth will be raised from death to life when the children of God are revealed (Ro 8: 19-21). When the covenant of peace is consummated, "the mountains and the hills before you shall break forth into singing, and all the trees of the field shall clap their hands." (Isa 55: 12)[146]

It's also important to stress the fact that this intermediate state is different for those who don't put their trust in Christ. Explaining this in a story, Jesus calls this reality a place of consuming fire, dryness, and sadness. (Matthew 10:28, 25:46, 2 Thess 1:9, et. al.) While this is a completely uncomfortable thought to dwell upon (and it should be) it's nonetheless critical to remember. Jesus lived, died, and rose to save us *from* something. That something is the eternal consequence for our temporal rebellion.

What is the difference between the intermediate state and our ultimate future hope?

RESURRECTION AND JUDGMENT

Jesus will return. Though we know this will happen, we don't know when. Jesus himself said that no one knows the day or the hour (Matthew 24:36), but it's an event that no one will miss.

> *And then they will see the Son of Man coming in clouds with great power and glory. And then he will send out the angels and gather his elect from the four winds, from the ends of the earth to the ends of heaven.* (Mark 13:26-27)

At some point in the timeline of this earth and heavens, Jesus will come back to the planet in much the same manner in which he left.[147] The intermediate state comes to an end at the return of Christ. This is the moment that Paul described when he wrote:

---

[146] Horton, Michael S. *The Christian Faith: A Systematic Theology for Pilgrims on the Way* (Kindle Locations 24367-24372). Zondervan. Kindle Edition.

[147] *And while they were gazing into heaven as he went, behold, two men stood by them in white robes, and said, "Men of Galilee, why do you stand looking into heaven? This Jesus, who was taken up from you into heaven, will come in the same way as you saw him go into heaven.* (Acts 1:10-11)

Chapter Nine – Hope

> *Behold! I tell you a mystery. We shall not all sleep, but we shall all be changed, in a moment, in the twinkling of an eye, at the last trumpet. For the trumpet will sound, and the dead will be raised imperishable, and we shall be changed.* (1 Corinthians 15:51-52)

While there's some fuzziness on the exact order of events (because of the nature of apocalyptic language) it's clear that Jesus Christ will return physically, powerfully, and stunningly. At that moment, the dead rise and the living and the dead are judged. And the judgment Jesus will render will be based not on the scales of our good and bad deeds, nor the winds of opinion and popularity. We will be judged on whether or not we trusted and followed Jesus.

What exactly does that mean? How is that fair? A million questions come rushing into our minds. Frantically, and quite naturally, we grab for reasons that a final judgment *can't* be true. "Don't people deserve another chance?" "What about those who didn't understand?" Yet, the Bible speaks into our confusion if we have ears to hear. I said that we are judged based on one of two things: Jesus works, or ours.

> *For we must all appear before the judgment seat of Christ, so that each one may receive what is due for what he has done in the body, whether good or evil.* (2 Corinthians 5:10)

In a very academic, hostile culture, Paul also said:

> *The times of ignorance God overlooked, but now he commands all people everywhere to repent, because he has fixed a day on which he will judge the world in righteousness by a man whom he has appointed; and of this he has given assurance to all by raising him from the dead.* (Acts 17:30-31)

All by themselves, these verses appear to teach a judgment based on works. Do good, get good. Do bad, go to Hell. But, these aren't the only words on the matter. We understand that the Scriptures have clearly taught that, while we are judged on the basis of God's moral law, no one can possibly fulfill that law.[148] In unbelievable love and mercy, God sent Jesus to live the perfect human life that none of us could live,[149] so that our judgment would no longer be based on our works, but on the perfect life of Jesus on our behalf.[150]

In Christ, we are found to have perfect righteousness, because Christ's righteousness is perfect. And, if we think about it long enough, we all really long for the judgment of God. What sane person doesn't want evil to end, injustice to be punished, and

---

[148] *For all who have sinned without the law will also perish without the law, and all who have sinned under the law will be judged by the law.* (Romans 2:12)

[149] *Therefore, just as sin came into the world through one man, and death through sin, and so death spread to all men because all sinned–for sin indeed was in the world before the law was given, but sin is not counted where there is no law. Yet death reigned from Adam to Moses, even over those whose sinning was not like the transgression of Adam, who was a type of the one who was to com. But the free gift is not like the trespass. For if many died through one man's trespass, much more have the grace of God and the free gift by the grace of that one man Jesus Christ abounded for many. And the free gift is not like the result of that one man's sin. For the judgment following one trespass brought condemnation, but the free gift following many trespasses brought justification. For if, because of one man's trespass, death reigned through that one man, much more will those who receive the abundance of grace and the free gift of righteousness reign in life through the one man Jesus Christ Therefore, as one trespass led to condemnation for all men, so one act of righteousness leads to justification and life for all men.* (Romans 5:12-18)

[150] *Truly, truly, I say to you, whoever hears my word and believes him who sent me has eternal life. He does not come into judgment, but has passed from death to life.* (John 5:24)

the world to get what's coming to it? Faced with a world in rebellion, a world full of exploitation and wickedness, a good God must be a God of judgment.[151]

> *God is going to kick sex trafficking and genocide out of it. But there is a rub: he is more serious about it than we are. The spark that sets the wildfire lives in us; the root of the wicked tree is in our hearts; the poisoned spring from which the deadly waters flow is not just "out there," it is "in here." The problem is us.*[152]

There is a coming future for the people of God – those who have turned from sin, trusted Jesus to rewrite their story, and follow Christ – that is beyond our capacity to imagine. Its goodness and joy are so great that our words to describe it are laughably small. The coming future happiness is so real, so supernatural, that we'll never cease celebrating it for a thousand epochs of time. And, there is a coming future for the people of self – those who refuse to turn from sin, insistent on writing their own story – that is beyond our capacity to imagine. Its terror and loneliness are so great that our words to describe it are frighteningly small. The coming future darkness is so real, so vacuous, that it will never cease for a thousand epochs of time.

How is this just? How can modern people believe in the "lake of fire," visualized in Revelation,[153] or the burning hell spoken of repeatedly by Jesus himself?[154] I do not pretend that this is an easy doctrine. It is terrifying and troubling in the deepest possible way. And, perhaps that is the point. Perhaps the point of Hell, amongst other things, is the conclusion we are forced to draw. From Hell we can conclude that sin is real and terrible. We might also conclude that God is deeply committed to holiness. Or, that in the final sense, justice will be done, and all evil will be excluded from God's new world.

Read Matthew 7:21-23. What did Jesus say to those who called him "Lord," but didn't live their lives under his lordship?

_____

_____

_____

---

[151] Wright, *Surprised by Hope*. 181.

[152] Butler, Joshua Ryan. *The Skeletons in God's Closet: The Mercy of Hell, the Surprise of Judgment, the Hope of Holy War* (pp. 25-26). Thomas Nelson.

[153] Revelation 20:11-15

[154] See Daniel 12:2, John 3:18, 36, 5:28-29, 2 Thess 1:6-8, Matt 3:12, 25:41, Mark 9:48, and Rev 14:10-11

Chapter Nine – Hope

NEW HEAVENS, NEW EARTH

King Jesus has defeated the kingdom of darkness. Think of it like this: when humanity rebelled against God, heaven and earth were ripped apart – like a garment torn in two. When the new heavens and the new earth come, heaven collides with this world, making all things new.

> *Then I saw a new heaven and a new earth, for the first heaven and the first earth had passed away, and the sea was no more. And I saw the holy city, new Jerusalem, coming down out of heaven from God, prepared as a bride adorned for her husband. And I heard a loud voice from the throne saying, "Behold, the dwelling place of God is with man. He will dwell with them, and they will be his people, and God himself will be with them as their God. (Revelation 21:1-3)*

Notice in the vision that John records: Heaven coming down to earth. Earth isn't just being destroyed, it's being remade. Wright explains:

> [W]hen we come to the picture of the actual end in Revelation 21-22, we find not ransomed souls making their way to a disembodied heaven but rather the new Jerusalem coming down from heaven to earth, uniting the two in a lasting embrace.[155]

This isn't some disembodied, ethereal, ghost-like world. This is a real, physical world with supernatural, heavenly possibilities. Imagine the difference between black and white TV and an IMAX theater. There is a massive, qualitative difference, and it will be better than we can possibly imagine.

Why?

Because God is there. He's *there*. No longer will God be hidden. No longer will God be invisible. No longer will God feel distant. He will be there, and so will we. We can't possibly realize all that will mean, but let's give it a try. Everything good that we experience in this life – laughter of children, delicious food, lovely art, amazing design – all points to some kind of source of goodness. Everything beautiful points to a source of beauty. Everything lovely points to a source of love. In the coming future, we live with the source. And no eye has yet seen, nor ear heard, nor mind imagined, what God has prepared for those who love him.[156]

How does this doctrine affect life? First, we come to see that this world really does matter. The work we do, the redemption we seek, the good we enjoy, it will last. It won't fade away, but be amplified, echoing into eternity. Secondly, we see that our world will be made new. All injustice, all sadness, all brokenness, all disease, all of it will eventually be done away with. And finally, we can have joy. If there really is a world coming in which all evil is destroyed, all injustice made right, and all things bright and beautiful are amplified into eternity, then very little in this life can make us very sad for very long.

---

[155] Wright, *Surprised by Hope*. 42.

[156] 1 Corinthians 2:9

What encourages you about the coming of the Kingdom of God? What, if anything, unsettles you?

_____

_____

_____

PATIENCE, HOPE, LONGING, AND LOVE

The end of the story is coming, but it's not here yet. The doctrine of the end of things makes us patient for God's future, and slow to believe the programs that promise to make heaven happen without him. Whatever professor, politician, or power-monger promises to bring utopia, they're wrong. We can be patient for God's future.

Furthermore, we can hope. We hold fast to the hope that we've received[157] because our hope is secure, even if this life isn't. Simultaneous with our hope, we can long for a better world. The gospel gives us the power and the permission to truly trust that the future is better and truly hate that it isn't yet.[158]

And finally, because we know that the future is coming, we can spend ourselves loving God and others, knowing we will receive a reward that is better than life. If this life is all there is, then really and relentlessly loving is impossible. In the final analysis, loving (which is giving yourself for the sake of another) is foolish, if there is no future. But because the gospel tells us that there is a world coming where those who loved most are most full, we can freely love now, even if it costs us everything.

And I think that's the point. I wish so much for your life and doctrine to collide like heaven and earth one day will. How deeply I desire that you would experience, along with me, the fullness of all hope in Christ, the pleasures of his brotherhood, the fellowship of God's fatherhood, and the friendship of his Spirit. Hope in God, for in him is the only fount and foundation of hope.

---

[157] *Let us hold fast the confession of our hope without wavering, for he who promised is faithful.* (Hebrews 10:23)

[158] *They cried out with a loud voice, "O Sovereign Lord, holy and true, how long before you will judge and avenge our blood on those who dwell on the earth?" Then they were each given a white robe and told to rest a little longer, until the number of their fellow servants and their brothers should be complete...* (Revelation 6:10-11)

Chapter Nine – Hope

QUESTIONS TO CONSIDER

1. What do you believe about the future? How is that different than what was outlined in this chapter?

2. The author wrote, "Christians have hope for the future because the future has come rushing backwards into the now – into history, in fact – in the resurrection of Jesus. In that event, we see what future is actually coming. And it's already here, though not quite yet." What does that mean?

3. Read Ephesians 1:16-21. What is the power that Paul wants us to understand and experience?

4. In Luke 11:1-2, what did Jesus teach us to pray? What does that mean?

5. Does the gospel help you love and care about this life, or care less about this life and this world? Why?

6. Read the Scriptures on page 165. What should we expect as the timeline of history progresses?

Hope – **Chapter Nine**

7. According to 2 Corinthians 5:6 and Hebrews 9:27, what happens when we die?

8. Read Philippians 3:20-21. What will happen to our bodies if we trust in Christ? Where is our citizenship?

9. According to Romans 2:8, what can those who reject God expect? According to 1 Thessalonians 1:10, what does Jesus do for us?

10. What is the future for the world, according to Revelation 21:1-3?

11. How does the doctrine of the future affect your life?

Chapter Nine – Hope

SCRIPTURE

Ephesians 1:16-21   Revelation 20-21   2 Corinthians 5:6
Hebrews 9:27   Philippians 3:20-21   1 Corinthians 15

POSTLUDE

WHAT

Postlude – What

MOVE

So what do you do now? You move.

I see it like this: experiencing and meditating on the gospel compels you to move. You just won't be able to stay still – at least, not for long.

The truth is that God made you in his image. You fail to live up to that image, just like the rest of us. But God knows that, so he's come after you anyway. He's the hero conquering the enemy. He's the cure defeating the disease. He's the hope sustaining the suffering. He's the champion taking the title. He did all this to come after you, save you, and share with you all that he is and all that he has.

What grace – God is inviting you into relationship with him. That's where the story moves from truth to grace, from facts to faith. A God like that isn't to be merely acknowledged, like a hat tip to a bellman. He is to be known and experienced. In his mercy, he's inviting you to know him, be freed from sin, and be filled with his power and presence. And when that happens – when the truth and the grace of the gospel mingle in the human heart, we change.

We move.

Away from sin, toward God. The author of the book of Hebrews commends us when he writes:

> *Therefore, since we are surrounded by so great a cloud of witnesses, let us also lay aside every weight, and sin which clings so closely, and let us run with endurance the race that is set before us, looking to Jesus, the founder and perfecter of our faith, who for the joy that was set before him endured the cross, despising the shame, and is seated at the right hand of the throne of God. Consider him who endured from sinners such hostility against himself, so that you may not grow weary or fainthearted.* (Hebrews 12:1-3)

Notice the kind of movement the Scriptures are asking of us. It's not walking or wandering, nor journeying or stumbling. It's running. We run from everything that separates us from right doctrine and right living. We run from all the good things that distract us from the right thing. We run from every tempting siren that promises happiness only to devour us. Run from all of that and run with all our might toward Jesus. He ran through it all for us. Now we can run through it all with him, and for him.

As with any kind of movement, we get tired after a while. Our bodies become weak, and we need rest. Weariness overtakes our good intentions, and we succumb to apathy. The Scriptures know that, too. That's why we're encouraged, "Consider [Jesus] … so you don't grow weary or fainthearted." Think on him, talk to him, picture him, worship him, and keep going after him.

Don't just move – run.

GO

There's one more kind of movement the Scriptures ask of us. We're not just to move toward God but toward people, too. Jesus said as much in his Great Commission:

> *Go therefore and make disciples of all nations, baptizing them in the name of the Father and of the Son and of the Holy Spirit, teaching them to observe all that I have commanded you. And behold, I am with you always, to the end of the age.* (Matthew 28:19-20)

If we really want to run after God, then we've got to run after others.

This is the call to those seeking to live gospel doctrines. This is life for those whose confession is also their obsession – to know Jesus at all costs, and to happily pay the cost for others to know him, too. Isn't this what God has done for us? Hasn't he willingly laid down the life of his beloved Son to obtain his lost people? What motivated God to do this? According to the passage in Hebrews we just read, it was, "for the joy set before him." For *his* joy.

That's mind-blowing. Jesus endured all the shame of the cross – the beatings, the mocking, the scourging, and the nails – because he was radically committed to getting all his joy in redeeming us.

Now he invites us to share that joy, as we go after him and others.

So, let's go.

FOR FURTHER

READING

In my journey, I've found it helpful to know what my favorite writers, speakers, and leaders have read — what shaped them. So, I composed a (very) partial list of some of the books that have shaped me. I hope you find them helpful.

- *Knowing God,* J.I. Packer
- *Mere Christianity,* C.S. Lewis
- *Can We Still Believe the Bible?,* Craig Blomberg
- *How to Read the Bible for All Its Worth,* Gordon Fee
- *Delighting in the Trinity,* Michael Reeves
- *Systematic Theology,* Wayne Grudem
- *How Long, O Lord?* D.A. Carson
- *The Doctrine of the Knowledge of God,* John Frame
- *WikiChurch,* Steve Murrell
- *Let the Nations be Glad,* John Piper
- *The Reason for God,* Timothy Keller
- *Where the Conflict Really Lies,* Alvin Plantinga
- *Inerrancy,* Norman Geisler
- *From Eden to New Jerusalem,* T. D. Alexander
- *The Christian Faith,* Michael Horton
- *Desiring God,* John Piper
- *Systematic Theology,* John Frame
- *Institutes of the Christian Religion,* Calvin
- *The Purple Book,* Murrell and Broocks
- *Holy Fire,* R. T. Kendall